BROKE VEGAN
SPEEDY

OVER 100 BUDGET PLANT-BASED RECIPES IN 30 MINUTES OR LESS

SASKIA SIDEY

First published in Great Britain in 2021 by Aster,
an imprint of Octopus Publishing Group Ltd
Carmelite House
50 Victoria Embankment
London EC4Y 0DZ
www.octopusbooks.co.uk
www.octopusbooksusa.com

An Hachette UK Company
www.hachette.co.uk

Distributed in the US by Hachette Book Group
1290 Avenue of the Americas
4th and 5th Floors
New York, NY 10104

Distributed in Canada by Canadian Manda Group
664 Annette St.
Toronto, Ontario
Canada M6S 2C8

ISBN 978 1 78325 4842

A CIP catalogue record for this book is available
from the British Library.

Printed and bound in The Czech Republic

13 5 7 9 10 8 6 4 2

Commissioned by George Brooker
Copy Editor: Lucy Bannell
Deputy Art Director: Jaz Bahra
Photographer and Props Stylist: Jo Sidey
Food Stylist: Saskia Sidey
Production Manager: Lisa Pinnell

Standard level spoon measurements are used in all recipes.
1 tablespoon = one 15 ml (½ fl oz) spoon
1 teaspoon = one 5 ml (⅙ fl oz) spoon
Imperial and metric measurements have been given in all recipes.
Use one set of measurements only and not a mixture of both.

CONTENTS

INTRODUCTION

We all want to save money, save the planet and, ultimately, save time. *Broke Vegan: Speedy* is here to help you do just that.

Every dish in this book takes no longer than 30 minutes to prepare, with lots that can be ready in just 5, 10 or 15 minutes. This book is designed so you can spend less time cooking, and more time sitting down to enjoy your delicious meal.

It's easier than you think to be a broke vegan. The trick is not to be fooled by too many meat and dairy replacements – these often come with a hefty price tag, while also being majorly over-processed, even ultra-processed, foods. So the recipes in this book don't use any tofu, tempeh, seitan, veggie sausages, vegan cheese or yogurt and the like. There's so much delicious food that can be made simply with vegetables, grains, pulses and seasonings that there's honestly just no need to bother with over-processed foods.

Vegan food often gets conflated with lofty 'wellness' pre-packaged ingredients, so many of the elements in 'healthy' vegan recipes end up racking up a big bill. While, of course, eating more vegetables is better for you and for the world, you won't find any chia, flax or hard-to-pronounce flours, seeds, powders or grains in these pages.

A FEW NOTES ON HOW TO STAY *SPEEDY*

Read through the recipe before you begin. I cannot stress this enough. There are often bits of prep that are outlined in the ingredients list, and you don't want to get caught out by suddenly needing a chopped onion.

As soon as you read that the oven needs to be on, get it on! Most ovens only take 10–15 minutes to heat up, but the longer the better for consistent cooking times.

Gather all your ingredients and equipment before you start cooking – this sounds obvious, but you'll save so much time if you're not having to dig around in your cupboards while your meal is bubbling away.

Try and tidy up as you go – whenever you have a moment when something is simmering or baking, take that time to wash up and wipe down; you'll thank yourself later.

TIME-SAVING TIPS

- When you have the oven on, make the most of its heat and minimize your power bill by roasting some extra veggies, such as squashes and root vegetables, for your meal, or baking some potatoes.

- If you know what you're making and have read through the recipe in advance, you'll have basically already cooked it in your head, saving you bags of time.

- Leftovers – repurposing leftovers means you're halving the initial effort and doubling your flavour output.

- Use the packaging that your produce comes in as containers while you're cooking, to save on washing up.

- If you are going to need hot stock quickly in a recipe, boil the kettle before you start cooking.

- Using canned pulses and pouches of ready-cooked grains isn't cheap; you can do it yourself far more economically and cooking them ahead will save you heaps of time. Cook a big batch of rice, grains or pulses yourself and freeze them in portion- or meal-sized sandwich bags to save the extra cash.

- Use the smallest number of pans that you possibly can. Think about how you can minimize washing up: if you can boil veggies and pasta in the same pan, do it!

- Use your common sense for ingredient swaps – it's better to use a lime in place of a lemon than wasting time going out to buy a lemon.

STORECUPBOARD ESSENTIALS

In order to make the most of the cheapest ingredients, there are certain storecupboard staples worth investing in. Although some of them may seem expensive when you first buy them, they'll last for months and add buckets of flavour to all your dishes.

PANTRY FLAVOUR-BOMBS

Capers
Chilli oil/chilli sauce
Dijon mustard
Green olives
Harissa paste
Maple syrup
Miso paste
Nutritional yeast
Tahini
Vanilla extract
Vegan bouillon powder
Yeast extract (such as Marmite)

FROZEN

OK, fine, your freezer isn't a cupboard, but it *is* a huge help in your cheap-eating arsenal. It makes your life easier and cooking faster when you've got a store of frozen goods that don't need to be defrosted to chuck into dishes. Always be on the lookout for deals in the supermarket. Reduced items almost past their expiration date or fruit and vegetables that look a little sad, that's where you can save so much money.

FREEZER FAVOURITES

Bread
Cooked rice and grains
Frozen fruit such as blueberries, blackberries and tropical fruits
Hash browns
Oven chips
Over-ripe bananas
Peas
Pesto
Spinach

PRE-PREPPED

I suggest chopping, portioning and freezing the following ingredients whenever you can buy them in bulk, or you have some produce that you think is at the end of its useful life. They can just be chucked into a pan straight away, as they'll mainly be used as the bases for soups, stews and sauces.

Carrots
Celery
Chilli
Garlic
Ginger
Onions

FLAVOUR BOMBS

When making a meal in a hurry, you want to think about how you can get maximum flavour without slaving over the stove. My favourite flavour boosters are:

Onion powder and garlic powder – for instant flavour hits without carefully cooking an onion, always keep these on hand (1 tablespoon onion powder = 1 chopped onion and ½ teaspoon garlic powder = 2 garlic cloves).

Marmite or yeast extract instantly gives slow-cooked depth of flavour and rich umami taste.

Celery salt – use it instead of salt for ragus and stews for another level of taste.

Dried mushrooms – either soaked or crushed, these give a real meatiness to vegan dishes.

Tahini – adds a creamy, rich and complex element to Middle Eastern and Asian dishes.

Tomato purée – a little goes a long way, and make sure to cook it out for a minute or so before adding any liquid to a dish.

Smoked paprika – my go-to spice, this can bring even a dull dish alive. So if you ever taste a cooking dish and are underwhelmed, reach for this.

Vegan bouillon powder – I always tend to use more of this than suggested on the back of the packet – go for a low-salt version if you're worried about the sodium content, but these powders are hyper-concentrated flavour bombs.

Nutritional yeast – nicknamed 'nooch' – is hardly a novel concept for the vegan community, but it is crucial for adding a funky cheesiness to dishes.

Miso paste – salty, savoury, zingy: perfect.

Crispy onions – buy these in big bags at Asian supermarkets. They're crunchy, salty and will last in an airtight container for what feels like forever.

FRESH

You should never be without:

Lemons and limes – citrus zest and juice is one of the easiest ways to elevate your dishes. They add brightness and cut through fat to make really harmonious and delicious food.

Ginger – warm, gently spicy and fresh. No need to bother peeling – grating this on a Microplane grater makes light work of the skin.

Garlic – a little trick to quickly peel garlic is to bash it with the heel of your hand to slightly dislodge the skin – you should find it then comes off easily in a single piece.

Alliums – red onions, white onions, spring onions and shallots all bring so much flavour, so mix them up, layer them in dishes or pick your favourite.

Dairy-free milk – this is the exception to my 'no dairy replacements' rule, because as long as you don't buy big named brands, it's a cheap and indispensable ingredient. I find that soy, almond and oat milks are pretty interchangeable, so when 'dairy-free milk' is called for in a recipe, just use your favourite.

WEEKDAY
LIFESAVERS

TERIYAKI COURGETTES

These are lovely served with stir-fried vegetables and noodles and also great simply over a bed of rice with some broccoli. You can of course use shop-bought vegan teriyaki sauce and shave off a few extra minutes from the cooking time.

SERVES 2

2 courgettes
1 tablespoon vegetable oil
250 g (8 oz) packet of
    microwaveable rice
150 g (5 oz) frozen peas or
    edamame beans

Teriyaki sauce
1½ teaspoons cornflour
100 ml (3½ fl oz) light soy
    sauce or tamari
100 ml (3½ fl oz) vegetable
    stock or water
4 tablespoons light brown or
    caster sugar
1 tablespoon rice vinegar,
    white wine vinegar or lime
    juice
1 garlic clove, finely grated
1 teaspoon finely grated fresh
    root ginger
1 teaspoon sesame oil

To serve
1 lime, quartered
1 red chilli, finely sliced
1–2 spring onions, finely
    sliced
1 tablespoon sesame seeds
    (optional)

Mix the cornflour with 2 tablespoons water and set aside.

Put the remaining teriyaki sauce ingredients in a saucepan and bring to the boil. Whisk in the cornflour mixture and simmer for 3–5 minutes until thickened, stirring regularly.

Halve the courgettes lengthways, then score a cross-hatch pattern in the flesh side. Toss in the vegetable oil and place flesh-side down in a large frying pan. Cook for 5–6 minutes until deeply golden, then flip and coat with a few tablespoons of the teriyaki sauce. Cover the pan with a lid and cook for a further 5 minutes until the courgettes are tender.

Reheat the rice according to the packet instructions.

Defrost the peas or edamame beans under running tap water. Toss them through the rice and top with the teriyaki courgettes, along with any extra sauce. Serve with the lime, red chilli, spring onions and sesame seeds, if you like.

CHICKPEA CURRY

This chickpea curry, inspired by the Caribbean flavours of Trinidad, is absolutely stunning, and very similar to a dhal. Best served with some roti or flatbread for scooping.

SERVES 2

2 tablespoons flavourless oil

3 garlic cloves, finely grated

1 red chilli, finely grated or chopped

1 onion, chopped

leaves from a few thyme sprigs

1 teaspoon ground cumin

1 teaspoon ground turmeric

I teaspoon dried fenugreek (optional)

1 tablespoon curry powder

400 g (13 oz) can of chickpeas, drained and rinsed

250 ml (8 fl oz) vegetable stock

small handful of coriander leaves, roughly chopped (optional)

salt and pepper

Heat the oil in a large heavy-based saucepan, then add the garlic, chilli and onion. Fry for 2–3 minutes until beginning to soften, then add the thyme, spices and a splash of water to prevent the spices from scorching. Fry for a further 2–3 minutes.

Add the chickpeas and stock and season well. Cover and cook for 10–15 minutes until the sauce has thickened.

At this point, you can use a stick blender to mash up some of the curry to give it a thicker texture, or remove a small amount and mash with a fork before returning it to the curry.

Sprinkle with coriander, if using, and serve.

GRATED CARROT, BEETROOT & ORANGE SALAD

You can add lots more shreddable veggies to this salad – try celeriac, kohlrabi and even a bit of apple. Serve with boiled potatoes as a main meal, or as part of a bigger spread.

SERVES 4

250 g (8 oz) carrots, peeled
250 g (8 oz) beetroot, peeled
2 oranges
2 teaspoons cumin seeds
1 teaspoon caraway seeds
2 tablespoons olive oil
finely grated zest and juice of
   1 lemon
small handful of mint leaves,
   roughly chopped
small handful of dill, roughly
   chopped
salt and pepper

Use a box grater or julienne peeler to shred the carrots and beetroot. Use a small serrated knife to remove the skin and membrane from the oranges, then slice into rounds and then half moons.

Toss the vegetables and oranges in a large salad bowl with the spices, oil, lemon zest and juice and herbs. Season well and serve.

HARISSA CORN SALAD

Harissa is a fantastic condiment to have on hand to add instant flavour to dishes. It's a sweet, spicy and rich chilli paste – if you don't have any, you could use another chilli paste, or try adding freshly chopped red chillies and a pinch of caraway seeds. Pictured on page 13.

SERVES 2

2 corn cobs, or 1 x 200 g
   (7 oz) can of sweetcorn,
   drained
1 red pepper, finely sliced
1 tablespoon harissa paste
1 tablespoon red wine
   vinegar
2 tablespoons olive oil
150 g (5 oz) couscous
1 tablespoon vegan bouillon
   powder
150 g (5 oz) cherry tomatoes,
   quartered
½ cucumber, finely chopped
 large handful of parsley
   leaves, roughly chopped
salt and pepper

Set a large dry frying pan over a high heat, add the corn and red pepper and cook, turning regularly, for 3–4 minutes until slightly charred. Take off the heat.

If using corn cobs, now slice the kernels from the cobs. To do this, set the cobs on their ends in a roasting tin and run a sharp knife down their lengths. Add the kernels, harissa paste, vinegar and oil to your salad bowl and stir to combine. Set aside.

Put the couscous in a bowl, cover with boiling water and sprinkle over the bouillon powder. Stir to combine and cover with a tea towel or some clingfilm and allow it to steam – around 3 minutes.

Toss the couscous with the cherry tomatoes, cucumber and parsley and top with the corn and red peppers. Season and serve.

CORONATION CHICKPEA SANDWICH

*This mildly spiced, gloriously sweet filling is awesome in a baked potato too.
It comes together in a flash. Saving chickpea water to make your own mayo seems
like a faff, but it honestly couldn't be easier. Pictured on page 17.*

*The vegan mayo recipe is a staple in my refrigerator and lasts for up to two weeks.
Making your own vegan mayo saves you so much money on the pre-packaged
stuff and it takes less than five minutes to whip up. Try adding lemon juice, stirring
through herbs or adding garlic to make aioli.*

**MAKES 2, WITH
LEFTOVERS**

400 g (13 oz) can of
   chickpeas, drained, liquid
   reserved
25 g (1 oz) raisins or sultanas
5 tablespoons vegan
   mayo (or see below for
   homemade)
1 tablespoon mango chutney
2 teaspoons mild curry
   powder
½ teaspoon ground cinnamon
salt and pepper

Vegan mayo (makes 1 jar)
50 ml (2 fl oz) aquafaba
   (reserved chickpea can
   liquid)
2 teaspoons Dijon mustard
1 tablespoon white wine
   vinegar, or to taste
200 ml (7 fl oz) flavourless
   oil

To serve
1 crusty baguette, halved
salad leaves
1 lime, cut into wedges

For the vegan mayo, place all the ingredients into a tall
container, season well and use a stick blender to combine
until thick and creamy – it should take 1–2 minutes.

Alternatively, if you only have a food processor, whizz
together the aqua faba, mustard, vinegar and seasoning,
then slowly drizzle in the oil through the spout while the
motor is running. Season to taste, adding more vinegar
if needed.

Place the chickpeas and sultanas in a bowl. Add the
mayo, chutney and spices and mix to thoroughly coat
the chickpeas. Season generously.

Place a few tablespoons of filling into the baguette with
some salad leaves and enjoy with a squeeze of lime juice.

LEFTOVER BURGER PATTIES

**MAKES 2 LARGE
PATTIES OR 6 SMALL
FRITTERS**

*Serve these crispy little burger patties in buns with lettuce,
mango chutney, sliced cucumber and chilli sauce, or serve
on their own as fritters.*

150 g (5 oz) leftover
Coronation Chickpea
Sandwich filling (see
page 15)
small handful of coriander
leaves, finely chopped
2 tablespoons gram flour or
plain flour, plus extra if
needed
flavourless oil, to fry

Mash the Coronation Chickpea filling with a fork or potato
masher so there are no whole chickpeas remaining. Mix with
the coriander and gram flour. You should be able to form it into
2 larger patties or 6 small fritters, but you can add a little more
flour if it makes the mix easier to handle.

Set a frying pan over a medium heat and add enough oil to
cover the base of the pan. Fry the patties for 2–3 minutes on
each side until crisp and golden.

OPPOSITE: CORONATION CHICKPEA SANDWICH

HUEV-NO RANCHEROS

Speedy refried beans are so hearty and warming – an epic breakfast that easily translates to a quick supper. Excessive amounts of hot sauce are optional here, but highly recommended. You could also knock up a quick tomato salsa with red onion, coriander and lots of lime juice for an extra zingy side.

SERVES 2

1 tablespoon olive oil
½ red onion, finely chopped
1 teaspoon ground cumin
1 teaspoon garlic powder
1 teaspoon smoked paprika
400 g (13 oz) can of black
 beans
finely grated zest and juice
 of 1 lime
2 flour or corn tortillas
salt and pepper

To serve
½ avocado, finely sliced
a few coriander sprigs
 (optional)
1 green chilli, finely sliced,
 or 2 tablespoons pickled
 jalapeños
hot sauce

Heat the oil in a nonstick frying pan and add the red onion. Cook for 5 minutes until softened, then add the spices and cook for 1 minute before adding the black beans, with the liquid from their can.

Simmer for 10 minutes, occasionally stirring, and use the back of a wooden spoon to mash down around half of the beans to thicken up the sauce.

Season well with the lime zest and juice, salt and pepper.

Microwave the tortilla wraps on high for 30 seconds. Serve the black beans over the tortillas with avocado slices, coriander, if using, chilli and as much hot sauce as you can handle. You can also slice the lime you used for juice and zest into wedges to serve, if you like.

TOMATO & AUBERGINE DIP

This tangy dip makes a welcome change from the more common baba ghanoush. It's incredibly comforting. Serve with plenty of soft pitta bread to mop it all up.

SERVES 2-4

4 tablespoons olive oil, plus
    extra to serve
1 large aubergine, peeled and
    cut into small cubes
3 tomatoes
4 garlic cloves
1 teaspoon ground coriander
½ teaspoon ground cumin
½ teaspoon chilli powder
small handful of parsley
    leaves, finely chopped,
    plus extra (optional) to
    serve
80–100 ml (3–3½ fl oz) water
1 tablespoon tomato purée
1 lemon, halved, 1 half sliced,
    to serve
salt and pepper
handful of green olives,
    roughly chopped, to serve

Put the olive oil in a heavy-based saucepan and add the aubergine. Halve and, using a box grater, grate the tomatoes directly into the pan, discarding the skin (which should be left when you get to the end). Grate in the garlic on the fine side of the grater. Add the spices, parsley and measured water and cover. Simmer until mushy, stirring regularly to break down the aubergines, around 20 minutes.

Stir through the tomato purée and the juice of ½ lemon, then simmer for a further 5–10 minutes. Season to taste.

Serve with olives, an extra drizzle of olive oil, the lemon slices and some extra parsley, if using.

VEGGIE COUSCOUS

The smaller you cut your veggies, the quicker they'll cook, so bear that in mind as you're chopping.

SERVES 2

1 red onion, chopped
1 red pepper, chopped
1 yellow pepper, chopped
1 courgette, chopped
1 carrot, chopped
2 tablespoons olive oil
1 teaspoon ground cumin
1 teaspoon ground cinnamon
1 teaspoon garlic powder
100 g (3½ oz) couscous
1 teaspoon vegan bouillon
    powder
½ teaspoon ground turmeric
50 g (2 oz) raisins
finely grated zest and juice of
    1 lemon
salt and pepper

To serve (optional)
handful of flaked almonds
handful of coriander, parsley
    or mint leaves, roughly
    chopped (optional)

Preheat the oven to 200°C (400°F), Gas Mark 6.

Toss the chopped vegetables with the olive oil, cumin, cinnamon and garlic powder. Season well and roast for 15–20 minutes until softened and beginning to char.

Meanwhile, put the couscous in a bowl with the bouillon powder, turmeric and raisins. Cover with boiling water, stir to combine, then cover with clingfilm or a tea towel and leave to stand for 10 minutes.

Fluff up with a fork, season with lemon zest and juice, salt and pepper, then top with the roasted veggies. Serve with almonds and herbs, if using.

FREEZER-FRIENDLY BURRITOS

FALAFEL-SPICED CAULIFLOWER

MAKES 4–6

1 red onion, finely sliced

400 g (13 oz) can of
chickpeas, drained and
rinsed

½ head of cauliflower,
chopped into very small
florets

2 teaspoons garlic powder

2 teaspoons ground cumin

1 teaspoon ground coriander

2 tablespoons olive oil

finely grated zest and juice of
½ lemon

large handful of parsley
leaves, very finely chopped

large handful of coriander
leaves, very finely chopped

4–6 large tortilla wraps

4–6 heaped tablespoons of
hummus

salt and pepper

Spend 30 minutes one day making yourself a tray-baked freezable burrito and thank yourself again and again when you can eat well whenever you want. Reheat the frozen burritos in a preheated oven at 180°C (350°F), Gas Mark 4 for 20–25 minutes until warmed through, or remove from their foil, wrap in damp kitchen paper and microwave on high for two or three minutes. These could make four, five or six burritos depending on the size of the tortilla wraps.

Preheat the oven to 220°C (425°F), Gas Mark 7.

Put the red onion, chickpeas, cauliflower, spices and oil in a large baking tray and toss well to combine. Season well and roast for 20–25 minutes until softened and beginning to blister.

Remove from the oven and stir through the lemon zest and juice, parsley and coriander.

Microwave the tortilla wraps on high for 30 seconds (this helps them be more malleable). Divide the filling between the tortilla wraps, add a dollop of hummus to each, then fold in the sides and roll up into tight logs.

Wrap the burritos in foil and freeze.

To reheat, preheat the oven to 180°C (350°F), Gas Mark 4. Place on the middle shelf for 20–25 minutes until piping hot in the middle.

SWEET POTATO & BLACK BEAN

MAKES 4-6

2 tablespoons olive oil

1 red onion, finely sliced

1 large sweet potato,
chopped into small cubes

1 tablespoon chipotle paste
or taco seasoning

400 g (13 oz) can of black
beans, drained and rinsed

200 g (7 oz) cherry
tomatoes, quartered

4-6 large tortilla wraps

hot sauce, to taste (optional)

salt and pepper

The more hot sauce you can handle the better for these smoky chipotle burritos – they are incredibly warming and satisfying.

Preheat the oven to 200°C (400°F), Gas Mark 6.

Toss the oil, onion, sweet potato and chipotle paste on a large baking tray, season well and roast for 15–20 minutes until the sweet potato is tender. Remove from the oven and stir through the black beans and cherry tomatoes.

Microwave the tortilla wraps on high for 30 seconds (this helps them be more malleable). Divide the filling between the tortilla wraps, add hot sauce if you like, then fold in the sides and roll up into tight logs.

Wrap the burritos in foil and freeze.

To reheat, preheat the oven to 180°C (350°F), Gas Mark 4. Place on the middle shelf for 20–25 minutes until piping hot in the middle.

CURRIED SWEET POTATO

MAKES 4-6

2 tablespoons olive oil

1 large sweet potato,
    chopped into small cubes

1 red onion, finely sliced

1 red pepper, chopped

1 tablespoon curry powder

2 teaspoons ground cumin

large handful of coriander
    leaves, very finely chopped

1 tablespoon lime juice

150 g (5 oz) frozen peas

4-6 tortilla wraps

salt and pepper

You can swap the sweet potato here for butternut squash or white potato.

Preheat the oven to 200°C (400°F), Gas Mark 6.

Toss the oil, sweet potato, red onion, red pepper and spices on a large baking tray, season well and roast for 15–20 minutes until the sweet potato is tender. Remove from the oven and stir through the coriander, lime juice and frozen peas.

Microwave the tortilla wraps on high for 30 seconds (this helps them be more malleable). Divide the filling between the tortilla wraps, then fold in the sides and roll up into tight logs.

Wrap the burritos in foil and freeze.

To reheat, preheat the oven to 180°C (350°F), Gas Mark 4. Place on the middle shelf for 20–25 minutes until piping hot in the middle.

BREAKFAST BURRITOS

MAKES 4-6

500 g (1 lb) button
    mushrooms, quartered or
    halved, depending on size
2 tablespoons oil
8-12 frozen hash browns
200 g (7 oz) jar of sun-dried
    tomatoes, drained
4-6 tortilla wraps
large handful of basil leaves,
    finely chopped
salt and pepper

Truly one of the easiest, but most delicious breakfasts you could hope to have in store. This tastes like a breakfast pizza, and that is a wonderful thing. The sun-dried tomato paste is a real instant flavour hack – you'll have loads leftover, so you can either freeze it to use another time or save it to make Pitta Pizzas (see page 52).

Preheat the oven to 220°C (425°F), Gas Mark 7.

Toss the mushrooms in the oil and put them on a baking sheet with the hash browns. Season well and roast for 20 minutes until the mushrooms have significantly shrunk and the hash browns are golden.

Meanwhile, blitz the sun-dried tomatoes in a food processor or with a stick blender until you have a smooth paste.

Microwave the tortilla wraps on high for 30 seconds (this helps them be more malleable).

Spread the sun-dried tomato paste on each tortilla wrap, sprinkle over the basil, divide the mushrooms between them and top each with 2 hash browns – depending on the shape, you may need to cut these to fit neatly. Fold in the sides and roll up into a tight log.

Wrap the burritos in foil and freeze.

To reheat, preheat the oven to 180°C (350°F), Gas Mark 4. Place on the middle shelf for 20–25 minutes until piping hot in the middle.

CORN & BEAN TAQUITOS

These flute-like stuffed tortilla rolls are often also called flautas – you will typically find them deep-fried, but I think that shallow frying yields results that are just as tasty. You'll get the crispiest taquitos if you use corn tortillas rather than wheat. You can also bake them at 180°C (350°F), Gas Mark 4 for 15–20 minutes for a healthier, more hands-off version. Try filling them with sweet potato or peppers, too.

SERVES 4–6

400 g (13 oz) can of black
    beans, drained and rinsed
200 g (7 oz) can of
    sweetcorn, drained
2 teaspoons ground cumin
2 teaspoons chipotle paste
½ small red onion, finely
    chopped
3 garlic cloves, finely grated
small handful of coriander
    leaves, finely chopped
juice of ½ lime
10–12 small tortillas (ideally
    corn, not wheat)
flavourless oil, to fry
salt and pepper

To serve
1 avocado
finely grated zest and juice
    of 1 lime
¼ lettuce, shredded
½ small red onion, finely
    chopped
1 tomato, finely chopped

In a large bowl, mash the beans with a potato masher or the back of a fork until mostly broken up. Add the sweetcorn, spices, onion, garlic and coriander. Mix well to combine. Season with salt, pepper and the lime juice.

Heat the tortillas for 30 seconds on high in the microwave (this helps them be more malleable).

Spread the filing down one end of the tortillas, and roll up very tightly, placing them seam-side down on a plate or tray while you repeat with the rest.

Add enough oil to a large frying pan to cover the base. Add the taquitos and cook seam-side down for 1–2 minutes, then flip and cook for another 1–2 minutes. Repeat until you have cooked them all.

Mash the flesh of the avocado with the zest and juice of the lime and season to taste.

Serve the taquitos with the mashed avocado, lettuce, onion and tomato.

INSTANT MINESTRONE

OK, not quite instant, but ready in the time it takes to cook your pasta.
The vegetables are all very interchangeable here – try asparagus,
cherry tomatoes, fennel or peas too. For even quicker prep, you could
grate all the vegetables, but the texture of some sturdier veg is lovely.

SERVES 4

100 g (3½ oz) small pasta,
   such as macaroni or ditalini
2 tablespoons olive oil, plus
   extra to drizzle
1 celery stick, finely sliced
1 carrot, halved and finely
   sliced
1 courgette, halved and finely
   sliced
1 large tomato
400 g (13 oz) can of borlotti
   beans
600 ml (1 pint) vegetable
   stock
2 teaspoons Marmite or other
   yeast extract
100 g kale (3½ oz), ribs
   removed, leaves roughly
   torn
salt and pepper

Bring a large pan of water to the boil. Salt it well and cook the pasta until al dente.

Meanwhile, in a separate deep saucepan, heat the oil, celery and carrot and cook over a high heat for 2 minutes until fragrant. Add the courgette and grate the tomato directly in using a box grater, discarding the skin that will remain.

Cook for 5 minutes, then add the can of beans, plus their liquid. Add the stock, Marmite and kale.

When the kale is wilted and tender, add the drained pasta. Season well. Serve with an extra drizzle of olive oil and enjoy.

CHICKPEA OMELETTE WITH MUSHROOM, SPINACH & TOMATO

Gram or chickpea flour is an incredible tool in your vegan arsenal. It has a slightly nutty flavour and, when cooked properly, can yield a custardy and soft result that just isn't possible with plain flour. If you're a fan of vegan cheese, try sprinkling some over the omelette before flipping, but I love it without. This recipe makes two omelettes, but you may want to cook them simultaneously in two pans in order to eat them at the same time. Pictured on page 33.

SERVES 2

Filling
1 tablespoon olive oil
200 g (7 oz) chestnut
   mushrooms, sliced or
   quartered
2 large handfuls of spinach
large handful of cherry
   tomatoes, halved
salt and pepper
small handful of parsley
   leaves and dill (optional)

Omelette batter
100 g (3½ oz) gram flour
¼ teaspoon ground turmeric
¼ teaspoon garlic powder
¼ teaspoon bicarbonate of
   soda
2 tablespoons nutritional
   yeast
175 ml (6 fl oz) dairy-free
   milk
2 teaspoons apple cider
   vinegar
1 tablespoon flavourless oil,
   to fry

Heat the olive oil in a nonstick frying pan and add the mushrooms. Fry for 5 minutes until golden. Add the spinach and tomatoes and cook until the spinach is wilted. Season well, then remove from the pan and set aside.

Sift the gram flour, spices and bicarbonate of soda into a large bowl. Add the nutritional yeast, then slowly add the dairy-free milk and apple cider vinegar, whisking constantly, until you have a smooth batter. Season with salt.

Heat the flavourless oil in the same nonstick frying pan you used for the mushrooms until the oil shimmers. Add half the batter to the pan and swirl to evenly coat the base. Cook for 2–3 minutes until starting to look brown and crispy on the bottom and dry on top – lots of small holes will appear over the surface. Add half the filling, then fold the omelette in half.

Turn the heat off, cover with a lid or foil and let the omelette steam for 5 minutes. Repeat the process with the second half of the batter.

Serve with a sprinkling of herbs, if you like.

SPRING OMELETTE

SERVES 1

½ quantity Chickpea Omelette batter (see page 31)

Filling
1 tablespoon vegan butter or
    margarine
1 small courgette, finely
    sliced
4 asparagus spears, halved
    lengthways
large handful of peas
small handful of mint
    leaves, roughly chopped
    (optional), to serve
salt and pepper

Perfect for the change of season when all the gorgeous green vegetables begin to flourish. If you can find asparagus on sale when it's in season, it's way cheaper. If you can't find asparagus cheaply, green beans will do.

Heat the butter in a nonstick frying pan and add the courgette and asparagus. Cook for 2–3 minutes until softened and beginning to gain some colour. Add the peas and stir to combine. Season well, remove from the pan and set aside.

Make the omelette as in the main recipe (see page 31), filling with the peas, courgette and asparagus and sprinkling with mint, if using.

SPICY ROLL UPS

SERVES 1

½ quantity Chickpea Omelette
    batter (see page 31)

Filling
1 tablespoon olive oil
1 teaspoon cumin seeds
½ teaspoon ground turmeric
½ teaspoon ground coriander
1 teaspoon curry powder
½ onion, finely chopped
1 garlic clove, finely grated
200 g (7 oz) green beans,
    sliced to 5 mm (¼ inch)
small handful of coriander
    leaves, roughly chopped
    (optional), to serve
salt and pepper

This omelette rolled around the vibrant green beans is more of a visual appeal than anything – if you don't feel confident rolling, just fold in half as above.

Heat the oil in a nonstick frying pan and add the spices and onion. Cook for 2–3 minutes until softened and beginning to gain some colour. Add the garlic and green beans and stir to combine. Season well and cook for 5 minutes until the green beans have softened. Remove from the pan and set aside.

Make the omelette as in the main recipe (see page 31), filling with the green bean mixture then rolling the omelette into a spiral before covering the pan and allowing it to steam. Slice and serve sprinkled with coriander, if using.

OPPOSITE: CHICKPEA OMELETTE WITH MUSHROOM, SPINACH & TOMATO

PEANUT BUTTER BEAN CURRY

This is one of the fastest curries imaginable to pull together. It's got a silky-smooth sauce and is lovely and mild. Incredibly comforting. Swap the butter beans for any bean – it works particularly well with chickpeas.

SERVES 4

1 tablespoon olive oil
1 onion, finely sliced
2 garlic cloves, finely grated
1 teaspoon ground coriander
1 teaspoon ground ginger
½ teaspoon chilli flakes
2 tablespoons tomato purée
5 tablespoons peanut butter
2 x 400 g (13 oz) cans of
   butter beans, drained and
   rinsed
400 ml (14 fl oz) can of
   coconut milk
1 tablespoon soy sauce
finely grated zest and juice
   of 1 lime
200 g (7 oz) fresh spinach or
   5 cubes of frozen spinach
salt

Heat the olive oil in a deep heavy-based saucepan. Add the onion and cook without colour for 5 minutes until translucent, then add the garlic and spices. Cook for a further minute until fragrant.

Add the tomato purée and cook for 1 minute until it deepens in colour, then add the peanut butter, butter beans, coconut milk and soy sauce.

Cook for 10 minutes until the curry has thickened slightly. Season with lime zest and juice and salt. Add the spinach, stir until it wilts down, then serve.

SAAG CHANA

This spinach and chickpea curry is incredibly rich and unctuous, and more similar to a saag paneer than traditional saag chana – blitzing the spinach and onion mixture makes all the difference: giving a silky-smooth sauce rather than chunks of spinach that stick in your teeth. It sounds like a lot of spinach, but it wilts down to nothing. Try serving it over a bed of rice or with naan bread.

SERVES 2

3 tablespoons olive oil

2 tablespoons coriander seeds

2 teaspoons cumin seeds

¼ teaspoon ground cardamom

½ teaspoon garam masala

1 onion, finely chopped

2 garlic cloves, finely grated

15 g (½ oz) fresh root ginger, finely grated

450 g (14½ oz) spinach

1 green chilli, halved, seeds removed (optional)

juice of 1 lime

50–100 ml (2–3½ fl oz) water

400 g (13 oz) can of chickpeas, drained and rinsed

Heat the olive oil in a large frying pan over a medium heat. Add the coriander and cumin seeds, cardamom and garam masala and cook until fragrant – about 1 minute. Add the onion and cook for 5 minutes until softened and translucent.

Add the garlic and ginger and cook for a further minute. Add the spinach and cook until it has just wilted. Don't cook it for too long, or it will lose its vibrant green colour.

Remove from the heat and put in a blender with the chilli and lime juice. Add the measured water and blitz until smooth.

Return the spinach purée to the pan, add the chickpeas and cook for 5 minutes until the chickpeas are thoroughly warmed through.

PEANUT & SWEET POTATO CURRY

This thick, rich, peanutty curry, inspired by the flavours from Thailand, uses a vegan shop-bought curry paste, which saves you a lot of time and effort searching for hard-to-source ingredients such as galangal and lemongrass. Make sure you buy a vegan curry paste, as some commercially available brands contain shrimp. If you don't have peanuts, just use double the amount of crunchy peanut butter.

SERVES 3–4

2 tablespoons panang or red
  curry paste
200 g (7 oz) sweet potato or
  carrots, chopped
400 ml (14 fl oz) can of
  coconut milk
1 tablespoon soy sauce
2 x 400 g (13 oz) cans of
  butter beans, drained and
  rinsed
2 tablespoons peanut butter
2 tablespoons raw peanuts,
  finely chopped
1 red pepper, chopped
1 yellow or orange pepper,
  chopped
150 g (5 oz) green beans,
  halved
juice of 1 lime
pinch of sugar (optional)
salt

Put the curry paste in a large saucepan and cook for 1 minute until the oil starts to separate. Add the sweet potato or carrots and cook for 5 minutes until beginning to soften. Add the coconut milk and soy sauce, bring to the boil and cook for 5 more minutes. Now add the butter beans and peanut butter with most of the chopped peanuts, reserving a few for the end. Cook for a further 10 minutes, then add the peppers and green beans. Cook for 5 minutes.

Season with the lime juice and salt, adding a pinch of sugar, if you like.

Serve with rice and scatter with the remaining chopped peanuts.

PLENTIFUL PORRIDGE

LEEK, MUSHROOM & MISO

SERVES 2

100 g (3½ oz) oats
700 ml (1 pint 3½ fl oz) water
   or vegetable stock
½ leek, finely sliced
150 g (5 oz) button
   mushrooms, sliced
1 head of pak choi, quartered
2 tablespoons flavourless oil
1 garlic clove, finely grated
2 teaspoons miso paste
1 tablespoon soy sauce
2 teaspoons mirin
1 tablespoon sesame seeds
salt

Savoury porridge for the win. Swap the pak choi for cabbage, or leave it out entirely. This is quite a filling breakfast that doubles up as a deeply comforting lunch. Pictured on page 39.

Put the oats and measured water or stock in a deep saucepan and cook, stirring every so often, for 8–10 minutes.

In a separate pan, fry the leek, mushrooms and pak choi in the oil over a medium heat until softened and beginning to gain some colour. Add the garlic and cook for a further minute until fragrant. Take off the heat and set aside.

Once the oats have absorbed almost all of the water but are still nicely soupy, add the miso, soy sauce and mirin. Season to taste with salt.

Pour the porridge into bowls, top with the sautéed veggies and sprinkle over the sesame seeds.

CREAMY SPINACH & CARROT

SERVES 2

100 g (3½ oz) oats
350 ml (12 fl oz) vegetable
    stock
350 ml (12 fl oz) dairy-free
    milk
1 carrot, grated
100 g (3½ oz) spinach
1–2 tablespoons nutritional
    yeast, to taste
salt and pepper

Mild, creamy and delectable. Try swapping the spinach for chard or kale for a more robust eat.

Gently heat the oats, stock and dairy-free milk in a saucepan, stirring regularly until all the liquid has been absorbed and the oats are creamy and tender – 8–10 minutes.

Stir through the grated carrot and spinach until the carrot softens slightly and the spinach wilts, 1–2 minutes.

Season to taste with nutritional yeast, salt and pepper and serve.

GINGER & SOY

SERVES 2

100 g (3½ oz) oats
700 ml (1 pint 3½ fl oz)
    vegetable stock
1 tablespoon soy sauce
1 teaspoon sesame oil
15 g (½ oz) fresh root ginger,
    sliced
2 spring onions, finely sliced
2 tablespoons crispy onions
1 tablespoon crispy chilli oil
    (optional), to serve
salt and pepper

This is exactly the kind of dish you want when you're feeling a little bit under the weather. Comforting and delicate.

Put the oats and stock in a deep saucepan. Add the soy sauce, sesame oil and ginger and cook, stirring every so often, for 8–10 minutes.

Once the oats have absorbed almost all of the water but are still nicely soupy, season to taste.

Pour the porridge into bowls, top with the spring onions and crispy onions and drizzle over the crispy chilli oil, if using.

OPPOSITE: LEEK, MUSHROOM & MISO

SWEET POTATO 'BRUSCHETTA'

This crispy baked bruschetta couldn't be easier and you can really go to town with the customizations. Tomato is a total classic, but you could try topping them with smashed peas and mint or guacamole and salsa.

SERVES 2–4

2 sweet potatoes, about
    400 g (13 oz), cut into
    5 mm (¼ inch) discs
4 tablespoons olive oil
200 g (7 oz) tomatoes,
    roughly chopped
½ small red onion, finely
    chopped
1 tablespoon balsamic
    vinegar or red wine
    vinegar
large handful of basil leaves,
    roughly chopped
½ garlic clove
salt and pepper

Preheat the oven to 200°C (400°F), Gas Mark 6.

Toss the sweet potatoes with 2 tablespoons of the oil in a baking tray, spread out into a single layer and bake for 20–25 minutes.

In a bowl, toss the tomatoes, remaining olive oil, red onion and vinegar and season to taste. Stir through half the basil.

When the sweet potatoes are done, rub one side of the surface with the cut side of the garlic clove, then top with the tomato mixture, sprinkling with the reserved basil. Eat immediately.

TAHINI, GRAINS & COURGETTE

Smooth, creamy and nutty tahini is a perfect partner for these delicately spiced courgettes. Any grain works well here in place of the brown rice - couscous, rice, bulgur wheat, freekeh, whatever you fancy or have to hand.

SERVES 2

1 large courgette, cut into
    2 cm (¾ inch) chunks
2 tablespoons olive oil
1 teaspoon ground cumin
1 teaspoon ground coriander
250 g (8 oz) packet of
    microwaveable brown rice
30 g (1 oz) raisins, sultanas or
    dried cranberries
10 green olives, halved
3 tablespoons tahini
1 garlic clove, finely grated
finely grated zest and juice of
    1 lemon
salt and pepper
large handful of parsley
    leaves, roughly chopped
    (optional), to serve

Put the courgette and olive oil in a large frying pan. Cook over a high heat for 3–4 minutes until the courgette is tender and beginning to gain lots of colour. Add the cumin and coriander and cook for 1 minute until fragrant. Season well and set aside.

Reheat the rice according to the packet instructions.

Toss the raisins and olives with the rice and top with the courgette.

In a small bowl, mix the tahini, garlic and lemon zest and juice with 1–2 tablespoons water until you have a dressing-like consistency.

Pour the dressing over the courgettes and scatter with the parsley, if using.

READY IN 15

RED PEPPER PESTO PASTA

Jarred red peppers are the fastest way to add buckets of flavour to this pesto. It saves the faff involved in charring and peeling your own. If your jarred peppers come suspended in oil, use that oil instead of the olive oil in the recipe for a zero-waste hack.

SERVES 4

150 g (5 oz) roasted red
   peppers
50 g (2 oz) almonds or
   walnuts
2 garlic cloves
2 tablespoons nutritional
   yeast
finely grated zest and juice of
   1 lemon
100 ml (3½ fl oz) olive oil or
   red pepper jar oil
200 g (7 oz) pasta
salt and pepper

To serve
leaves from a few parsley
   sprigs, roughly chopped,
   to serve (optional)
Vegan 'Parmesan' (see page
   111, optional)

Put the red peppers, nuts, garlic and nutritional yeast in a food processor and blitz until broken down. Add the lemon zest and juice and slowly drizzle in the olive oil with the food processor running until you have a smooth and creamy pesto. Season to taste.

Boil the pasta for 8–10 minutes until al dente.

Toss through the pesto and scatter with parsley and Vegan 'Parmesan', if using.

PAN CON TOMATE

Ripe tomatoes here are key, so don't be trying to make this in the dead of winter. If you do have sea salt flakes and extra virgin olive oil, those will make all the difference too.

SERVES 2

2 large, ripe tomatoes
2 slices of rustic or
   sourdough bread
½ garlic clove
salt, ideally sea salt flakes
1 tablespoon olive oil, to
   serve

Halve the tomatoes. Set a sieve above a bowl and grate the tomatoes on the coarse side of a box grater into the sieve until only the skins remain – discard the skins. Allow the liquid from the grated tomatoes to drain away into the bowl and discard.

Toast the bread and rub it liberally with the cut side of the garlic clove.

Spread the tomato flesh over the bread, drizzle with oil and season well with salt.

BROCCOLI TEMPURA

These tempura greens work with anything – I love them with chard or green beans too. Blanching the broccoli means its super-tender inside, with a great crunch on the outside.

SERVES 2

200 g (7 oz) Tenderstem
   broccoli
25 g (1 oz) cornflour
75 g (3 oz) plain flour, plus
   extra for dredging
½ teaspoon salt
½ teaspoon sugar
125 ml (4 fl oz) soda water
flavourless oil, to deep-fry

Soy Vinegar Dipping Sauce
50 ml (2 fl oz) soy sauce
2 tablespoons rice vinegar or
   black vinegar
1 garlic clove, finely grated
1 teaspoon finely grated fresh
   root ginger
1 red chilli, finely chopped

Ponzu Mayo Dipping Sauce
5 tablespoons vegan mayo
   (for homemade, see
   page 15)
2 tablespoons soy sauce
2 teaspoons lemon juice
½ teaspoon ground ginger
salt and pepper

Bring a large pot of water to the boil. Blanch the broccoli for 1 minute, then drain and set aside on kitchen paper to dry.

To make both the dipping sauces, simply mix all the ingredients together in separate bowls. Season the ponzu mayo sauce.

Put both the flours, the salt and sugar in a mixing bowl. Slowly whisk in enough soda water until the batter is the consistency of double cream. Don't worry too much about lumps – little clumps in the batter turn extra crispy as you fry them. Put some flour in a separate shallow bowl.

Pour the oil into a wok to come halfway up the sides and heat to 180°C (350°F). If you don't have an oil thermometer, test the heat with the handle of a wooden spoon: when you put it in the oil, bubbles should immediately form around it.

Dredge the broccoli in the bowl of flour, then drop it in the batter. Remove the stems, shaking to remove excess batter, then drop them straight into the oil and cook for 2–3 minutes until golden and crisp.

Season the broccoli as soon as it comes out of the oil and serve with a choice of the dipping sauces.

CAULIFLOWER RICE RISOTTO

This super-fast supper makes light work out of the traditionally laborious risotto. Creamy, aromatic and rich, it is a low-carb and low-effort dish. You can swap the stock for any flavour soup for an instant upgrade – it's particularly nice with squash or pea soup.

SERVES 2

1 small cauliflower, broken into small florets (about 450 g/14½ oz)

1 tablespoon olive oil

1 banana shallot, or ½ onion, very finely chopped

2 garlic cloves, finely grated

leaves from 2 thyme sprigs, plus extra (optional) to serve

100 ml (3½ fl oz) white wine or vermouth

300 ml (½ pint) hot vegetable stock

2 tablespoons nutritional yeast

cracked black pepper, to serve

Pulse the cauliflower florets 6–8 times in a food processor until you have pieces that are lentil- or breadcrumb-sized. Don't leave it on for too long, or you'll end up with mush.

Put the oil in a high-sided frying pan and add the shallot. Sauté until softened and translucent, around 2 minutes. Add the garlic and thyme and cook for another minute.

Add the cauliflower rice to the pan and fry for 2 minutes until fragrant and just starting to brown. Add the white wine and let the cauliflower fully absorb it before proceeding to add the vegetable stock in 2–3 additions, waiting for the cauliflower to absorb most of the liquid before adding more.

Taste the risotto: the cauliflower should be tender but retain a bite. Season with nutritional yeast and turn off the heat. Allow to rest for a few minutes before serving with plenty of cracked black pepper and extra thyme leaves, if liked.

PEA & LEMON

SERVES 2

1 quantity Cauliflower Rice Risotto (see above)

150 g (5 oz) frozen peas

finely grated zest and juice of 1 lemon

This variation brings in fresh, spring flavours along with a burst of colour. Pictured on page 51.

Follow the instructions for the risotto as in the main recipe above, adding the frozen peas with the last addition of vegetable stock. Season with lemon zest and juice as you add the nutritional yeast.

PEA & LEMON

COURGETTE & TOMATO

SERVES 2

The fried courgette in this variation brings a great texture.

1 quantity Cauliflower Rice
Risotto (see page 50)
1 courgette, finely sliced
2 tablespoons olive oil
2 tablespoons sun-dried
tomato purée (see Pitta
Pizzas with Sun-dried
Tomatoes & Olives,
page 52)
salt and pepper

Before starting on the risotto, toss the courgette slices in the olive oil, season well and start to fry the courgettes in a large frying pan until golden – 5–10 minutes. While they cook you can begin the risotto.

Follow the instructions for the risotto as in the main recipe on page 50, adding the sun-dried tomato purée after the shallots and cooking for a further 1–2 minutes until the paste turns a deeper shade of red. Continue with the risotto as in the main recipe.

Top the risotto with the courgette slices and serve.

PITTA PIZZAS WITH SUN-DRIED TOMATOES & OLIVES

If you're a fan of vegan cheese, by all means add it here, but this recipe is still flavour town without it. The world is your vegan-oyster, so use whatever toppings you fancy. Keep any leftover sun-dried tomato paste in a jar in the refrigerator, or freeze for when you'll need it next.

MAKES 3

200 g (7 oz) jar of sun-dried
   tomatoes, drained
3 pitta breads
½ garlic clove, finely sliced
1 teaspoon dried oregano
2 tablespoons Vegan
   'Parmesan' (see page 111)
100 g (3½ oz) cherry
   tomatoes, halved
½ green pepper, finely sliced
50 g (2 oz) olives, halved
salt and pepper

To serve
small handful of basil leaves
   (optional)
1 tablespoon olive oil

Preheat the oven to 220°C (425°F), Gas Mark 7.

Blitz the sun-dried tomatoes in a food processor or with a stick blender until you have a smooth paste.

Lay the pitta breads on a baking tray. Spread 1 tablespoon sun-dried tomato purée on each pitta, followed by some garlic slices and a sprinkling of oregano and Vegan 'Parmesan'. Top with tomatoes, peppers and olives.

Bake for 10 minutes. Remove from the oven, season well and eat immediately, sprinkled with basil, if using, and olive oil.

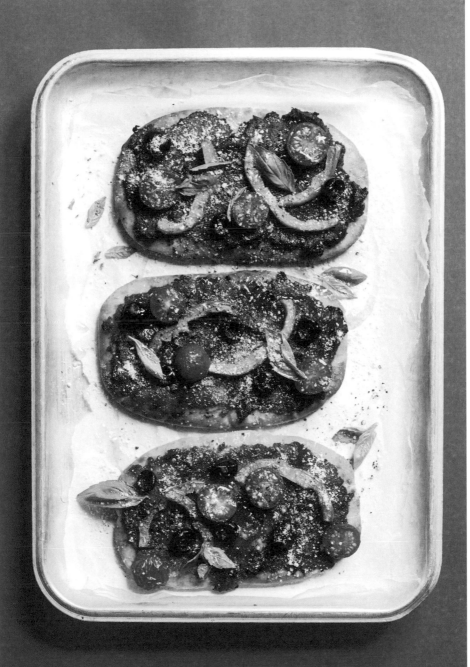

BROCCOLI STALK PESTO PASTA

A perfect waste-free dish to use up those broccoli stalks that you inevitably don't use as often as you should. If you don't have a broccoli stalk lying around, add some broccoli florets to the water at the same time as the pasta, for an extra green addition.

SERVES 2–4

1 large broccoli stalk, roughly
  chopped
50 g (2 oz) cashews
1 garlic clove
1 tablespoon nutritional yeast
  (optional)
finely grated zest and juice of
  1 lemon
large handful of soft herb
  leaves, such as basil,
  parsley or mint
100 ml (3½ fl oz) olive oil
200 g (7 oz) pasta of your
  choice
salt and pepper

Put the broccoli stalk in a food processor with the cashews, garlic and nutritional yeast, if using. Blitz for 2–3 minutes until broken down.

Add the lemon zest and juice and the herbs and season well. Blend until smooth, another minute or so. Slowly drizzle in the olive oil until you have a smooth and creamy pesto.

Boil the pasta for 8–10 minute until al dente.

Toss through the pesto and serve.

LAKSA

SERVES 1

1 tablespoon vegan laksa
    paste or red curry paste
1 tablespoon brown sugar
100 ml (3½ fl oz) coconut
    milk
350 ml (12 fl oz) boiling
    water
1 packet instant ramen
    noodles
juice of ½ lime

To serve
½ red chilli, finely sliced
2 tablespoons crispy fried
    onions
small handful of beansprouts
small handful of coriander
    sprigs (optional)

A packet of instant noodles really does mean there's no excuse not to have a flavour-packed lunch on the table in minutes. You'll want to put these crispy fried onions on everything, so snatch a big bag next time you're in a local Asian supermarket; they're so cheap, too.

Place a saucepan over a medium heat. Put in the laksa paste and brown sugar and cook for 1 minute, stirring constantly until the paste separates.

Add the coconut milk and the measured boiling water and bring to the boil. Add the noodles and their seasoning packets and cook for 2–3 minutes until the noodles are tender.

Season with the lime juice, then cut any leftover lime into wedges to serve.

Serve sprinkled with red chilli slices, crispy fried onions, beansprouts and coriander, if using, and with the lime wedges for squeezing over.

THAI GREEN NOODLE SOUP

SERVES 1

1 tablespoon green
    curry paste
100 ml (3½ fl oz) coconut
    milk
350 ml (12 fl oz) boiling
    water
1 packet instant ramen
    noodles
50 g (2 oz) green beans
juice of ½ lime
½ green chilli, finely sliced
handful of beansprouts
small handful of Thai basil
    or regular basil leaves
    (optional)

Curry paste is such a versatile ingredient and using a shop-bought one is actually cheaper than using homemade.

Place a saucepan over a medium heat. Add the green curry paste and cook for 1 minute, stirring constantly until the paste separates slightly.

Add the coconut milk and the measured boiling water and bring to the boil. Add the instant noodles, their seasoning packets and the green beans to the saucepan. Cook for 2–3 minutes until the noodles are tender.

Season with the lime juice, then cut any leftover lime into wedges to serve.

Sprinkle with chilli slices, beansprouts and basil, if using, to serve.

MISO RAMEN

SERVES 1

1 tablespoon white miso
    paste
1 tablespoon sesame oil
1 tablespoon soy sauce
1 packet instant ramen
    noodles
400 ml (14 fl oz) boiling
    water
handful of frozen edamame
    beans
1 spring onion, finely sliced
½ carrot, julienned or grated

If you don't have white miso paste but have a sachet of miso soup stashed in the cupboard, that's a great alternative here.

Place a saucepan over a medium heat. Add the miso paste, sesame oil and soy sauce and cook for 30 seconds before adding the ramen noodles and their seasoning packets with the measured boiling water.

Cook for 1 minute, then toss in the edamame beans and cook for a further 1–2 minutes until the noodles are tender, but still chewy.

Serve the noodles in the cooking broth with sliced spring onion and carrot.

VEGETABLE FRITTERS

COURGETTE

SERVES 2

1 large courgette
½ garlic clove, finely grated
4 tablespoons gram flour
2 tablespoons nutritional
  yeast
2 spring onions, finely
  chopped
small handful of dill, finely
  chopped
small handful of mint leaves,
  finely chopped
2 tablespoons olive oil
salt

These Greek-inspired courgette fritters use gram flour, which makes them simultaneously really crunchy on the outside and delightfully creamy and soft within. Delicious with tzatziki – you can make a quick version with vegan mayo or yogurt and a little grated cucumber, garlic, white wine vinegar, dill and mint.

Grate the courgette using the coarse side of a box grater directly into a sieve lined with a tea towel. Sprinkle with some salt, scrunch the courgette well with your hands to distribute, and leave for 10 minutes.

In a large bowl, put the grated garlic, flour, nutritional yeast, spring onions and herbs.

Pull the tea towel around the grated courgette and squeeze out as much of the moisture as you can (without being too crazy about it) and add to the bowl, mixing well to combine.

Add half the olive oil to a frying pan over a medium heat. Fry heaped tablespoons of the batter, in batches, for around 3 minutes on each side, turning once they are golden brown and visibly crisp. Add more oil and batter as needed. Drain on a piece of kitchen paper and season with an extra pinch of salt.

CARROT

SERVES 2

2 carrots
½ garlic clove, finely grated
4 tablespoons gram or
    chickpea flour
2 tablespoons nutritional
    yeast
2 spring onions, finely
    chopped
1 teaspoon garam masala
small handful of coriander
    leaves, finely chopped
2 tablespoons olive oil
salt

This is a pretty easy swap for the courgette – you could do a half-half mix, or also use the same recipe with sweetcorn and peas, it's very versatile. Adding garam masala and swapping the herbs for coriander give these a wonderful curried taste.

Follow the same method as for the Courgette Fritters on page 58, although it isn't necessary to squeeze any moisture from the carrots. Add garam masala and coriander in place of the other herbs.

SWEETCORN PANCAKES

SERVES 2

340 g (11½ oz) can of
    sweetcorn, drained
handful of spinach
1 garlic clove
75g (3 oz) gram flour
½ teaspoon baking powder
50 ml (2 fl oz) dairy-free milk
1 spring onion, finely sliced
small handful of coriander
    leaves, roughly chopped
2 tablespoons vegetable oil
salt and pepper

These soft and sweet pancakes are gorgeous served with chilli jam, guacamole or a tomato salsa.

Set 2 tablespoons of sweetcorn aside. Add the remaining sweetcorn to a blender with the spinach, garlic, flour, baking powder and dairy-free milk. Blitz until smooth.

Stir through the spring onion, coriander and reserved sweetcorn and season well.

Heat the oil in a large frying pan and fry the batter in batches until golden brown on both sides, about 2 minutes on each.

Serve and eat immediately.

SHREDDED RICE NOODLE SALAD

This salad has a tongue-tingling chilli oil dressing that you'll want to put on everything.

SERVES 2

150 g (5 oz) rice noodles

2 spring onions, finely sliced

1 carrot, grated or julienned

½ cucumber, grated or
    julienned

½ white cabbage, shredded
    (optional)

small handful of coriander
    and mint leaves, roughly
    chopped, plus extra
    (optional) to serve

Dressing

1 garlic clove, finely grated

4 tablespoons soy sauce

2 tablespoons lime juice

1 tablespoon light brown
    sugar

1 tablespoon sesame oil

2 tablespoons crispy chilli oil

salt

To Serve

2 tablespoons salted roasted
    peanuts

½ red bell pepper, finely
    sliced

Cover the rice noodles with boiling water and set aside.

Put all the vegetables and herbs in a large bowl. Mix together the dressing ingredients in a separate bowl, season to taste with salt, then pour over the vegetables.

Drain the rice noodles once tender and add to the bowl, tossing well to combine.

Serve sprinkled with extra herbs, if you like, peanuts and red pepper.

SMASHED PEAS ON TOAST

*To quickly defrost frozen peas, run them under water from the tap,
drain, and you're good to go. If you happen to have half an avocado
you don't know what to do with, adding it can make this really creamy.*

SERVES 2

2 slices of sourdough bread
200 g (7 oz) peas, fresh or
   frozen and defrosted
finely grated zest and juice
   of 1 lime
½ garlic clove, finely grated
small handful of mint leaves
small handful of coriander
   leaves
salt and pepper
1 tablespoon olive oil, to
   serve

Toast the bread.

Put the peas in a bowl and mash roughly half of them with
a potato masher or the back of a fork (you could also use
a stick blender for a creamier result). Stir through the lime
zest and juice, garlic, mint and coriander.

Heap the mashed pea mixture onto the toast, drizzle with
oil and season.

SPEEDY VEGGIE NOODLES

This is a perfect dish for those who only have access to a microwave, or anyone who's in a real hurry. The only work you need to do is chopping the veggies – or you could even buy a pre-prepared bag of stir-fry veg and avoid that step completely.

SERVES 1–2

2 tablespoons soy sauce

1 tablespoon caster sugar

1 tablespoon sriracha or other hot sauce

1 300 g packet of straight-to-wok pre-cooked noodles

½ head of broccoli, broken into florets

¼ red pepper, finely sliced

½ red onion, finely sliced

large handful of kale, ribs removed, leaves roughly torn

large handful of beansprouts

1 tablespoon sesame seeds, to serve

In a large microwave-safe container with a lid, mix the soy sauce, sugar and sriracha. Add the noodles, broccoli, red pepper and red onion. Pop the lid on and shake everything around to mix thoroughly.

Cook for 3 minutes on high in the microwave, stirring once. Add the kale and beansprouts and cook for a further 3 minutes.

Sprinkle with sesame seeds to serve.

BEETROOT HUMMUS RAINBOW WRAPS

This is a very lazy hack of simply blitzing beetroot with store-bought hummus and pumping up the flavour. Alternately, you could blitz the beetroot with chickpeas, garlic, lemon, tahini and olive oil to make your own from scratch. When you're buying pre-cooked beetroot, just make sure it's not pickled in vinegar or you'll have a very different-tasting dish!

SERVES 2

2 cooked beetroot

1 x 200 g (7 oz) tub of hummus

1 garlic clove

finely grated zest and juice of 1 lemon

2 large tortillas or wraps

1 avocado, sliced

1 carrot, coarsely grated

1 cucumber, finely sliced

large handful of spinach

salt and pepper

Put the beetroot, hummus, garlic and lemon zest and juice in a blender. Blitz until smooth.

Spread heaped tablespoons of the hummus along the centre of the tortillas, then top with avocado slices, grated carrot, cucumber and spinach leaves. Season well.

Wrap the tortillas, folding in the sides and rolling up into logs, and enjoy.

SAVOURY FRENCH TOAST

The crunch on this spiced French toast is insane. Savoury really is the word here – you'll be eating every last crumb, I promise. Try swapping the spices for smoked paprika and cumin and serving the toast with guacamole for a Mexican-inspired twist.

SERVES 2

50 g (2 oz) gram flour
125 ml (4 fl oz) dairy-free
    milk
½ teaspoon baking powder
1 teaspoon nigella or onion
    seeds (optional)
½ teaspoon ground turmeric
½ teaspoon ground cumin
2 slices of stale sourdough
    or any crusty bread
1 tablespoon olive oil or
    vegan butter
salt and pepper

Kachumber salsa
¼ cucumber, finely chopped
1 tomato, finely chopped
¼ red onion, finely chopped
2 tablespoons lime juice
small handful of coriander
    leaves, finely chopped,
    plus extra (optional) to
    serve

In a shallow bowl, mix together the gram flour, dairy-free milk, baking powder, spices and salt to taste. Soak the bread in the mixture, a slice at a time, until totally saturated.

Heat the olive oil or vegan butter in a frying pan and add the slices. Cook for 2–3 minutes on each side until golden, crisp and slightly puffy.

While the toast is cooking, mix together all the ingredients for the kachumber salsa and season to taste.

Serve the toast with the salsa and eat right away.

AGLIO E OLIO

Think of the chilli flakes here as a choose-your-own-adventure style.
As cooking the chilli amplifies the flavour, they can be particularly
fiery so be mindful of how spicy you like things when adding them or
leave them out completely. Top this with Vegan 'Parmesan', if you like.

SERVES 2

200 g (7 oz) spaghetti
4 tablespoons olive oil, plus
 extra to serve
4 garlic cloves, finely sliced
½–1 teaspoon chilli flakes
 (optional)
large handful of parsley
 leaves, finely chopped,
 plus extra to serve
finely grated zest and juice of
 ½ lemon
salt and pepper
Vegan 'Parmesan' (see page
 111, optional), to serve

Salt a large pan of boiling water generously, then add the spaghetti.

Meanwhile, put the oil into a frying pan and add the garlic. Turn the heat to medium and cook until fragrant and just starting to turn golden – around 1 minute. Add the chilli flakes and cook for 30 seconds. Take 1 ladleful of pasta water, add to the pan and simmer gently until slightly thickened.

Once the pasta is al dente, drain it and add to the pan with the parsley, lemon zest and juice. Toss vigorously until the pasta sauce is coating the spaghetti and it looks nice and glossy.

Serve with extra olive oil, parsley and Vegan 'Parmesan', if you like.

SESAME & PEANUT NOODLES

This is a simple storecupboard dish to pull together, but it's also really nice to sauté extra vegetables and toss them through with the noodles – try slicing red peppers, carrots, mushrooms and sugar snaps. You can also add a splash of coconut milk to make it extra creamy.

SERVES 2

200 g (7 oz) udon or any
   type of noodles
1 teaspoon garlic powder
2 teaspoons sesame oil
2 tablespoons peanut butter
juice of 1 lime
1 tablespoon soy sauce
½ teaspoon ground ginger
2 tablespoons water

To serve
1 tablespoon sesame seeds
2 spring onions, finely sliced

Bring a large pan of water to the boil and add the noodles. Cook for a few minutes until al dente, then drain.

Mix together the garlic powder, sesame oil, peanut butter, lime juice, soy sauce, ground ginger and measured water until you have a smooth sauce. Pour the sauce over the noodles and combine off the heat.

Serve sprinkled with sesame seeds and spring onions.

COLD AVOCADO NOODLES

When you're craving something salty, creamy and aromatic, this is just the ticket. If you like things extra spicy, add some crispy chilli oil or extra freshly sliced chillies too.

SERVES 2

150 g (5 oz) soba noodles

2 avocados

finely grated zest and juice
   of 1 lime

1 garlic clove, finely grated

1 teaspoon finely grated fresh
   root ginger

small handful of coriander
   leaves

1 tablespoon sesame oil

salt and pepper

To serve

1 red chilli, diced or a few
   pinches of chilli flakes
   (optional)

1 tablespoon sesame seeds
   (optional)

Bring a large pan of salted water to the boil and cook the noodles until al dente. Drain and run under cool water to stop the cooking.

While the noodles are cooking, scoop out the flesh of the avocados and add to a blender with the lime zest and juice, garlic, ginger and coriander. Blitz until smooth, adding 2–3 tablespoons of water if the mixture is not smooth or if your blender is struggling to mix it. Season.

Toss the avocado sauce with the sesame oil and noodles and sprinkle with diced chilli and sesame seeds, if you like.

ALL IN ONE

ROASTED TOMATO SOUP WITH QUICK GREMOLATA

Bung it all in, blitz it up and bliss out. This soup takes on other flavours really well. You could try adding some chillies and coconut milk instead of stock for a spicy alternative. Here, we're adding breadcrumbs to a gremolata to make it more of a crunchy topping than just the usual burst of lemon-and-herb freshness – it's fantastic scattered over the soup, and also over stews and pasta dishes. The garlic and parsley are optional, but try to use at least one of them.

SERVES 4

10–12 large vine tomatoes, halved
2 tablespoons olive oil, plus extra to drizzle
1 red onion, quartered
a few basil sprigs, plus extra leaves to serve
6 garlic cloves, in their skins
200–300 ml (7 fl oz–½ pint) hot vegetable stock
1–2 tablespoons balsamic vinegar
salt and pepper

Quick gremolata
50 g (2 oz) breadcrumbs
2 tablespoons olive oil
1 large garlic clove, finely grated (optional)
large handful of parsley leaves, finely chopped (optional)
finely grated zest of 1 lemon

Preheat the oven to 200°C (400°F), Gas Mark 6.

Put the tomatoes, oil, onion, basil sprigs and garlic in a deep roasting tray, season, then roast for 25 minutes until softened and blistered. Squeeze the garlic cloves from their skins and discard the skins and the basil sprigs. Take the outer leaf of the onion off if it appears too charred.

Meanwhile, for the gremolata, put the breadcrumbs and olive oil into a pan and cook for 1–2 minutes until the breadcrumbs are golden brown. Take off the heat and stir through the garlic and parsley, if using, and lemon zest. Season well.

Pour 200 ml (7 fl oz) of the hot stock into the roasting tray with the balsamic vinegar, then use a stick blender to whizz everything up until smooth – you can add more stock if you like it a bit looser. Season well, drizzle with olive oil and serve strewn with basil leaves and the gremolata.

ONE-POT PASTA

RED CABBAGE & MISO

SERVES 2

1 teaspoon white wine
    vinegar
½ red cabbage, shredded
150 g (5 oz) spaghetti or
    linguine
30 g (1 oz) vegan butter or
    margarine
1 tablespoon miso paste
3 garlic cloves, finely grated
finely grated zest and juice of
    1 lemon
salt and pepper
parsley leaves, to serve
    (optional)

*In this recipe, you use the pot first to boil the cabbage,
then boil the pasta in the same water – turning the pasta an
amazing shade of purple. Once drained, you'll use the pot to
make and combine the sauce with the pasta and cabbage.*

Bring a large pan of salted water to the boil and add the
vinegar. Drop in the red cabbage and cook for 2–3 minutes
until tender. Scoop out the cabbage and set aside, leaving the
water in the pan, and then cook the pasta for 8–10 minutes
until al dente. Reserve 1 cup of the pasta water, then drain.

Return the pan to a medium heat, melt the butter and miso
paste together, then add the garlic and fry for 1 minute
until fragrant. Add the reserved pasta water slowly, mixing
constantly to emulsify the sauce, and season well. Return the
pasta and cabbage to the pan and toss together to combine
until the pasta looks silky. Season with lemon juice, and scatter
with parsley, if you like, and lemon zest to serve.

CHERRY TOMATOES

SERVES 2

150 g (5 oz) spaghetti or
    linguine
1 shallot, very finely sliced
200 g (7 oz) cherry
    tomatoes, halved
2 tablespoons capers,
    drained
2 garlic cloves, finely grated
4 tablespoons olive oil
450 ml (¾ pint) boiling water
    or vegetable stock
salt and pepper
basil leaves, to serve
    (optional)

*It feels pretty magical that you can really just dump all the
ingredients into a pot and hope for the best with these one-pot
pasta dishes. Trust the measurements – it really works.*

Place all the ingredients except the basil in a large saucepan
(ideally wide enough so that the pasta can lie flat on the base),
cover and bring to the boil. Reduce the heat so the mixture is
gently simmering, then remove the lid and cook for 12 minutes,
stirring regularly to make sure the pasta isn't sticking.

Take off the heat, season well and toss vigorously to combine
until you have a silky-smooth sauce. Serve scattered with basil,
if you like.

PEA & SPINACH

SERVES 2

150 g (5 oz) spaghetti
2 garlic cloves, finely grated
4 tablespoons olive oil
80 g (3 oz) frozen peas
4 cubes of frozen spinach
250 ml (8 fl oz) boiling water
200 ml (7 fl oz) dairy-free
    milk
large handful of basil leaves,
    roughly chopped
2 tablespoons nutritional
    yeast
salt and pepper

*A perfect dish for when you feel like you've got nothing in the
refrigerator – a delicious reason always to have frozen peas
and spinach on hand.*

Place all the ingredients apart from the basil and nutritional
yeast in a large saucepan (ideally wide enough so that the
pasta can lie flat on the base), cover and bring to the boil.
Reduce the heat so the mixture is gently simmering, then
remove the lid and cook for 12 minutes, stirring regularly to
make sure the pasta isn't sticking.

Take off the heat, add the basil and nutritional yeast and
season well. Toss vigorously to combine until you have
a silky-smooth sauce, then serve.

LENTIL & TOMATO STEW

This budget-friendly warming stew comes together so quickly that you'll have plenty of time to relax, or to cut lots of crusty bread to mop it all up with.

SERVES 2–3

1 tablespoon olive oil
1 onion, finely chopped
2 garlic cloves, finely grated
2 teaspoons ground cumin
1 teaspoon ground cinnamon
250 g (8 oz) red lentils, rinsed
400 g (13 oz) can of chopped
   tomatoes
750 ml (1¼ pints) vegetable
   stock
juice of 1 lemon
salt and pepper
mint leaves, to serve (optional)

Heat a large, high-sided frying pan. Add the oil and onion with a pinch of salt and cook for 5 minutes until softened. Once the onion has softened, add the garlic, cumin and cinnamon and cook for 1 minute until fragrant.

Add the lentils, tomatoes and stock. Bring to the boil, then reduce the heat to a simmer and cook for 20 25 minutes. Season well with lemon juice, salt and pepper and serve scattered with mint leaves, if you like.

ROASTED CAULIFLOWER SOUP WITH CRUNCHY LEAF CROUTONS

Roasting cauliflower really enhances its nutty flavour in this rich, velvety soup. Cauliflower leaves are some of the tastiest greens available – more delicate than kale, they crisp up insanely well.

SERVES 4

1 cauliflower, broken into small florets, leaves reserved
4 tablespoons olive oil
1 onion, roughly chopped
leaves from 2 thyme sprigs
4 garlic cloves, finely grated
1.5 litres (2½ pints) vegetable stock
juice of ½ lemon
salt and pepper

Preheat the oven to 200°C (400°F), Gas Mark 6.

Place the cauliflower florets on a baking tray and toss with 2 tablespoons oil. Season well and roast for 20 minutes.

Meanwhile, in a large pan, cook the onion with 1 tablespoon oil, cooking it without colour for 5 minutes until translucent and soft. Add the thyme leaves and garlic and cook for 1 minute until fragrant. Pour in the stock and bring to a simmer.

When the cauliflower florets are browned, toss the cauliflower leaves with the remaining 1 tablespoon oil, season and roast for 5–10 minutes until crisp. Meanwhile, add the florets to the pan of stock and cook for 5 minutes.

Use a stick blender to whizz the soup until smooth. Season to taste with lemon juice and salt, then serve with the crispy leaf croutons.

ROASTED SPICY CAULIFLOWER SOUP

SERVES 4

1 quantity Roasted Cauliflower Soup with Crunchy Leaf Croutons (above)
1 tablespoon garam masala
1 teaspoon ground cumin
1 teaspoon ground coriander
large handful of coriander leaves (optional), to serve
1 teaspoon chilli flakes (optional), to serve

For when you need a little extra kick.

Follow the method for the cauliflower soup in the main recipe above, adding the garam masala, cumin and coriander with the thyme leaves.

Serve with the Crispy Leaf Croutons, coriander leaves and a sprinkling of chilli flakes, if you like.

AUBERGINE & POTATO CURRY

This is lovely served over rice with a scattering of coriander. The key is cutting the potatoes and aubergine small enough that they become tender in the short cooking time.

SERVES 2

1 aubergine, cut into small
  cubes
2 waxy potatoes (about
  500 g/1 lb total weight),
  cut into small cubes
1 onion, finely chopped
1 tablespoon finely grated
  fresh root ginger
2 tablespoons olive oil
1 tablespoon curry powder
1 teaspoon ground turmeric
400 ml (14 fl oz) can of
  coconut milk
200 g (7 oz) spinach or 100 g
  (3½ oz) kale, ribs removed,
  leaves roughly torn
1 lemon
salt
coriander leaves, to serve
  (optional)

Put the aubergine, potatoes, onion and ginger in a deep heavy-based saucepan with the oil. Sauté for 5 minutes, then add a mugful of water, cover and cook for 15 minutes, stirring occasionally.

When the aubergine and potatoes are tender, add the curry powder, turmeric and coconut milk. Bring to the boil, then stir through the greens. Season with lemon juice and salt.

Scatter with coriander, if using, and serve with rice.

GNOCCHI BAKE

ARRABIATA

SERVES 2

Fiery, spicy, and so dang easy that it's sure to become a staple in your recipe rotation.

3 tablespoons olive oil

2 garlic cloves, finely sliced

1 red chilli, finely chopped, or 1 teaspoon chilli flakes

400 ml (14 fl oz) tomato passata

½ teaspoon dried oregano

500 g (1 lb) packet of pre-cooked gnocchi

a few basil leaves (optional)

salt and pepper

½ lemon, cut into wedges, to serve

Preheat the oven to 180°C (350°F), Gas Mark 4.

Put the oil, garlic, chilli, passata and oregano in a deep baking dish and stir well to combine. Season well.

Add the gnocchi and toss to combine. Bake for 25 minutes until the sauce has thickened and it is beginning to colour in places on top.

Scatter with basil leaves, if using, and serve with lemon wedges.

GREEN CHILLI & LEMON

SERVES 2

This bake is so bright and fresh thanks to the knock-out combination of chilli and lemon. How many chillies you want to add – and whether you deseed them or not – will depend on how spicy they are: a trick is to nibble the very tip of the chilli, opposite to the stalk end; if you can't feel anything right away, they're probably not too hot.

3 tablespoons olive oil

2 garlic cloves

1–2 green chillies, halved

finely grated zest and juice of 1 lemon

100 g (3½ oz) spinach

1 tablespoon nutritional yeast

500 g (1 lb) packet of pre-cooked gnocchi

200 ml (7 fl oz) vegetable stock

To serve (optional)

1 green chilli, finely sliced

½ teaspoon chilli flakes

parsley and basil leaves

Preheat the oven to 180°C (350°F), Gas Mark 4.

Put the oil, garlic, chilli(es), lemon juice, spinach and nutritional yeast in a blender. Whizz up until smooth.

Scrape the mixture into a deep baking dish along with the gnocchi and stock and toss well to combine.

Bake for 20–25 minutes until the sauce has thickened and it is beginning to colour in places on top.

Scatter with lemon zest, extra chilli and herbs, if using.

CREAMY WHITE BEAN & KALE

SERVES 2

400 g (13 oz) can of
   cannellini beans, drained
   and rinsed

1 garlic clove

2 tablespoons nutritional
   yeast, plus extra to sprinkle

200 ml (7 fl oz) dairy-free
   milk

finely grated zest of 1 lemon

500 g (1 lb) packet of
   pre-cooked gnocchi

100 g (3½ oz) kale, ribs
   removed, leaves roughly
   torn

3 tablespoons breadcrumbs

small handful of parsley
   leaves, finely chopped
   (optional), to serve

Swap the kale here for spinach if you prefer. This is best eaten straight out of the oven, while the sauce is still super-creamy.

Preheat the oven to 180°C (350°F), Gas Mark 4.

Put the beans, garlic, nutritional yeast and dairy-free milk in a blender and blitz until smooth.

Pour the mixture into a deep baking dish and add the lemon zest, gnocchi and kale. Toss well to combine. Sprinkle with the breadcrumbs and extra nutritional yeast.

Bake for 20–25 minutes until the sauce has thickened and it is beginning to colour in places on top.

Scatter with the parsley, if using. You can also slice the lemon you used to zest into wedges to serve, if you like.

LENTIL 'RAGU'

If you want to save even more cash, you could cook a big batch of lentils and then freeze them in portions, but canned cooked lentils (rather than the trendy – and more expensive – pouches) can be really affordable too. If you don't have a food processor to help make quick work of the veggie chopping, try using a box grater instead. Serve this 'ragu' with pasta, or on top of quick polenta or mashed potato.

SERVES 4

1 onion, roughly chopped
1 leek, roughly chopped
1 carrot, roughly chopped
1 celery stick, roughly
   chopped
2 tablespoons olive oil
3 garlic cloves, finely
   chopped or grated
400 g (13 oz) can of green
   lentils in water, drained
500 g (1 lb) tomato passata
2 tablespoons vegan bouillon
   powder
1 tablespoon Marmite or
   other yeast extract
salt and pepper
small handful of basil leaves
   (optional), to serve

In a food processor, blitz the onion, leek, carrot and celery. You may want to do this in batches, depending on the size of your food processor.

Put the oil in a deep heavy-based saucepan over a medium heat. Add the chopped vegetables and sauté for 5–8 minutes until beginning to soften. Add the garlic and cook for a further minute.

Add the drained lentils, passata, bouillon and Marmite, bring to the boil, then reduce the heat to a simmer and cook for 20 minutes. While the 'ragu' is cooking, you can make some pasta, if you'd like. Season to taste and serve with basil leaves, if you like.

SPEEDY & SPICY NOODLE SOUP

Inspired by the flavours of Japanese katsu curry, this dish is delicately spiced and is finished off by the freshness of spring onions and coriander.

SERVES 2

2 tablespoons vegetable oil

1 onion, finely chopped

2 carrots, finely chopped

4 garlic cloves, finely grated

10 g (¼ oz) fresh root ginger, finely grated

1½ tablespoons curry powder

1 tablespoon vegan bouillon powder

2 tablespoons soy sauce

1 litre (1¾ pints) boiling water

150 g (5 oz) dried noodles

To serve

2 spring onions, finely sliced

a few coriander sprigs (optional)

a handful of beansprouts (optional)

Put the oil in a large pan and fry the onion and carrots over a low heat for 4–5 minutes until translucent and soft. Add the garlic and ginger and fry for 1 minute until fragrant, before adding the curry powder. Cook, stirring regularly, for 1 minute.

Add the vegan bouillon powder, soy sauce and measured boiling water. Bring to the boil, add the noodles and cook for 5–8 minutes until tender.

Sprinkle with the spring onions, coriander and beansprouts, if using, to serve.

PAPPA AL POMODORO

This simple soup is an amazing and hearty way to use up stale bread. It's best to use canned plum tomatoes instead of chopped – they're typically the higher-quality tomatoes for the same price.

SERVES 3-4

3 tablespoons olive oil, plus
    extra to serve
1 onion, finely chopped
5 garlic cloves, finely grated
3-4 basil sprigs, plus extra
    to serve
2 x 400 g (13 oz) cans of
    plum tomatoes
200 g (7 oz) stale bread,
    crusts removed, torn into
    small chunks
1 teaspoon sugar
2 teaspoons vegan bouillon
    powder
salt and pepper

Put the oil in a high-sided frying pan and sauté the onion for 5 minutes until softened. Add the garlic and basil sprigs and cook for 1 minute until fragrant.

Add the canned tomatoes, then fill one of the cans up with water and add this to the pan. Crush the tomatoes with the back of a wooden spoon and bring to a simmer.

Add the bread, sugar and bouillon powder and simmer for 15–20 minutes until the bread has broken down and the soup has thickened substantially – it won't have a traditional 'soup' consistency, think of it more like a porridge or stew.

Season well and serve with extra basil leaves and a drizzle of olive oil.

CURRIED SWEET POTATO DIP

This is smooth, buttery and completely addictive. You could even add
some vegetable stock to turn it into a soup.

SERVES 2-4

1 sweet potato (250–300 g/
8–10 oz), peeled and cut
into small cubes
1 large tomato, quartered
1 red onion, roughly chopped
2 tablespoons olive oil
1 teaspoon ground cumin
1 teaspoon curry powder
½ teaspoon chilli powder
juice of 1 lime
salt and pepper

Preheat the oven to 200°C (400°F), Gas Mark 6.

Toss the sweet potato, tomato and red onion with the oil
and spices. Roast for 20 minutes until the sweet potato
is tender.

Scrape into a food processor and blitz together, seasoning
with lime juice, salt and pepper.

Serve with tortilla chips, flatbreads or crudités.

A LITTLE BIT
SPECIAL

BARBECUE CORN RIBS

This has to be the most fun way to eat corn on the cob – they're like little riblets. You'll need a sharp knife and a bit of gumption to cut through the core. For a Middle Eastern vibe, try swapping the barbecue sauce for pomegranate molasses and dress with tahini. These cook in minutes on the barbecue instead of in the oven, if you have one.

SERVES 4 AS A SIDE DISH OR 2 AS A MAIN COURSE

4 corn cobs
2 tablespoon olive oil
4 tablespoons barbecue sauce
2 teaspoon onion powder
2 teaspoon garlic powder
1 teaspoon smoked paprika
salt and pepper

To serve
finely grated zest of 1 lime and juice of ½ lime
2 tablespoons vegan mayo (for homemade, see page 15)
small handful of coriander leaves
2 spring onions, finely sliced

Preheat the oven to 200°C (400°F), Gas Mark 6.

Microwave the corn cobs for 4 minutes on high to make them softer to work with. Trim the ends off each corn cob so they're flat on the base. Quarter the corn cobs lengthways through the core, to make 4 long, skinny wedges. Toss the wedges in the oil, barbecue sauce and seasonings.

Remove the cobs from the marinade (reserve the marinade), then roast them on a baking tray for 25 minutes until the cobs have curled, become golden and are starting to get blistered in places.

While the corn is roasting, add the lime zest and juice to the mayo.

Toss the cobs back in the marinade when they're just out of the oven, then drizzle with the lime mayo. Serve with the remaining lime half for squeezing, scattering over the coriander and spring onions.

CHIPS THREE WAYS

SATAY CRACKERS

**SERVES 4 AS A
STARTER OR NIBBLE**

family-sized bag of vegan
Thai-spiced crackers
1 carrot, peeled and finely
chopped
1 cucumber, finely chopped
1 red pepper, finely chopped

Sauce
2 tablespoons sweet chilli
sauce
2 tablespoons lime juice
3 tablespoons peanut butter
1 tablespoon soy sauce

To serve
2 spring onions, finely sliced
leaves from a few mint sprigs
leaves from a few coriander
sprigs
handful of roasted salted
peanuts, roughly chopped

*If you can't find vegan Thai-spiced crackers in your
supermarket (they're usually found near other crisps) you can
make your own with rice paper – cut it into chunky squares
and deep-fry in flavourless oil – it only takes 5 minutes and
couldn't be easier. For an extra kick, serve these nachos with
some extra sweet chilli sauce too.*

Mix together everything for the sauce in a small bowl until
smooth. If the sauce needs loosening, add a tablespoon of
water. Set aside.

Put the crackers on a platter and top with the finely
chopped vegetables.

Drizzle the sauce over the crackers, then scatter with the
spring onions, herbs and peanuts to serve.

LOADED POPPADOMS

**SERVES 4 AS A
STARTER OR NIBBLE**

2 tablespoons flavourless oil

1 tablespoon curry powder

1 teaspoon garlic powder

400 g (13 oz) can of
   chickpeas, drained and
   rinsed

family-sized bag of mini
   poppadoms, or a few large
   poppadoms broken into
   smaller pieces

1 red onion, finely chopped

2 tomatoes, finely chopped

handful of pomegranate
   seeds (optional)

2 tablespoons mango
   chutney (optional)

3 tablespoons vegan mayo
   (for homemade see
   page 15)

finely grated zest and juice
   of 1 lime

½ teaspoon ground cumin

leaves from a few coriander
   sprigs, to serve

*Applying the principle of nachos to everything in the snack
aisle seems to be a pretty solid bet. Crunchy, spicy, saucy
and addictive.*

Heat the oil in a frying pan and add the curry powder and
garlic powder with a splash of water to stop the spices
getting scorched. Cook for 1 minute until fragrant.
Add the chickpeas and cook for 5 minutes until crispy
and combined.

Spread out the poppadoms on a platter and top with the
curried chickpeas and the chopped vegetables, adding
the pomegranate seeds, if using.

In a small bowl, mix together the chutney, if using, vegan
mayo, lime zest and juice and cumin. Drizzle this over the
poppadoms and scatter with coriander leaves.

SWEET POTATO NACHOS

**SERVES 4 AS A
STARTER OR NIBBLE**

*Classic. The limey sweet potato purée here takes the place of
a more traditional nacho cheese sauce, and it's fabulous.*

1 sweet potato
finely grated zest and juice
    of 1 lime
hot sauce, to taste
400 g (13 oz) can of black
    beans, drained and rinsed
1 avocado, cut into small
    cubes
150 g (5 oz) cherry tomatoes,
    quartered
2 spring onions, finely sliced
family-sized bag of tortilla
    chips
2 tablespoons pickled
    jalapeños
small handful of coriander
    leaves

Prick the sweet potato with a fork and microwave on high
for 6–8 minutes until soft to the touch. Split in half and
allow to cool slightly, then scrape out the flesh and season
to taste with the lime zest and juice and the hot sauce.
Mash very well until smooth.

In a small bowl, mix together the black beans, avocado,
cherry tomatoes and spring onions, seasoning with any
remaining lime juice.

Lay the tortilla chips on a platter and top with spoonfuls
of the sweet potato mash, the black bean salsa, pickled
jalapeños and coriander leaves. Add extra hot sauce, to
taste, if you like.

WHITE BEAN CROQUETTES

These croquette-style patties are incredibly creamy – no one would believe they weren't made with a bechamel. They can be quite delicate, so take care when breadcrumbing them, but the softness pays off when you eat them! Serve with vegan mayo for dunking and a simply dressed salad for an amazingly easy but filling supper.

SERVES 2–4

1 tablespoon olive oil
2 shallots, finely sliced
2 garlic cloves, finely
    chopped or finely grated
leaves from a few thyme
    sprigs, roughly chopped
100 g (3½ oz) spinach
½ teaspoon smoked paprika
400 g (13 oz) can of
    cannellini or butter beans,
    drained, liquid reserved
150 g (5 oz) breadcrumbs
flavourless oil, to fry

Put the olive oil in a frying pan and set it over a low heat. Add the shallots and cook for 5 minutes until softened. Add the garlic and thyme and cook for another minute until fragrant. Add the spinach and cook until it has wilted. Stir through the paprika and beans (reserve the liquid from the can for now). Add 50 g (2 oz) of the breadcrumbs and stir to combine.

Use a stick blender to blitz until smooth, or scrape into a food processor. Pop the mixture into the freezer for 10 minutes to quickly cool down.

Put the cannellini bean liquid into one bowl and the remaining breadcrumbs into another. Take a heaped tablespoon of the spinach and bean mixture, drop it into the breadcrumbs and toss to coat – this will help you form it into a log shape. Then carefully coat in the bean liquid, then toss in the breadcrumbs again (this double coating helps them to stick together).

Heat a few tablespoons of flavourless oil in a frying pan, then fry the croquettes for 3–4 minutes on each side until golden.

CHICKPEAS BRAVAS WITH AQUAFABA AIOLI

This also works incredibly well with butter beans, which have a delightful texture, but chickpeas are chosen here to provide the aquafaba that you need to make your own aioli. By all means use shop-bought, if you're pinched for time. You can also go more traditional by par-boiling and then frying little cubes of potato to add to the chickpea mix.

SERVES 2

3 tablespoons olive oil

400 g (13 oz) can of chickpeas, drained, liquid reserved

1 onion, finely chopped

1 red chilli, finely chopped

1 teaspoon smoked paprika

400 g (13 oz) can of chopped tomatoes

2 teaspoons red wine vinegar or sherry vinegar

1 teaspoon sugar

salt and pepper

Aioli

1 quantity vegan mayo (for homemade see page 15)

½ garlic clove, finely grated

½ teaspoon garlic powder

To serve (optional)

parsley leaves, roughly chopped

1 tablespoon chives, roughly chopped

In a small frying pan, heat 2 tablespoons of olive oil and add the drained chickpeas (if you want them extra crisp, pat them dry with kitchen paper first). Season well and fry for 5 minutes until crisp and golden. Set aside.

To make the bravas sauce, heat the remaining 1 tablespoon oil in a separate larger frying pan, add the onion and chilli and cook without colour for 5 minutes until softened. Add the smoked paprika and cook for 1 minute. Add the canned tomatoes, vinegar and sugar, season well and simmer for 10–15 minutes until reduced. Taste and season: it should be sharp, sweet and spicy.

Mix the ingredients for the aioli in a small bowl, taste for seasoning.

To serve, top the crispy chickpeas with the spicy bravas sauce and aioli, scattering with plenty of parsley, if you like.

BUTTERNUT SQUASH ROSTIS

These make a weekend brunch feel a little more special and are so easy to make.

SERVES 2

½ small butternut squash,
    peeled and grated
½ onion, grated
3 tablespoons peanut butter
1 garlic clove, finely chopped
1 teaspoon ground cumin
1 teaspoon ground coriander
handful of mint, basil and
    parsley leaves, chopped,
    plus extra to serve
50 g (2 oz) plain flour
flavourless oil, to fry
salt and pepper
½ lemon, sliced into wedges,
    to serve

Put the grated butternut squash and onion into a microwave-safe bowl and cover with clingfilm. Cook on high for 2 minutes. Remove and pour off any liquid that has collected in the bowl.

Meanwhile, mix together the peanut butter, garlic, spices and herbs. Add the grated squash and onion, season and mix well.

Form the mixture into clementine-sized balls, and roll in the flour on a large plate.

Put enough oil into a large frying pan to coat the base and add 4–5 rosti balls at a time. Push down on them with the back of a spatula to make them more patty shaped and cook for 2–3 minutes on each side until golden and crisp. Serve with a scattering of extra fresh herbs and a lemon wedge.

STUFFED BABY AUBERGINES

Baby aubergines are perfect for quick suppers, as they're so much faster to cook than their big brothers. This filling is a sort of spicy baba ghanoush hybrid. Serve with a green salad.

SERVES 4

12 baby aubergines
2 tablespoons olive oil
2 tablespoons tahini
2 teaspoons harissa paste
finely grated zest and juice of
  1 lemon
large handful of parsley
  leaves, finely chopped,
  plus extra to serve
2 garlic cloves, finely grated
120 g (4 oz) couscous
salt and pepper
mint leaves, to serve
  (optional)

Preheat the oven to 200°C (400°F), Gas Mark 6.

Halve the aubergines and toss in the oil on a large baking tray, then roast, cut-sides down, for 20 minutes until tender.

In the meantime, mix together the tahini, harissa, lemon juice and zest, parsley and garlic.

Pop the couscous in a bowl and cover with boiling water. Cover with clingfilm or a tea towel for 10 minutes until tender. Stir in the tahini mixture.

When the aubergines are tender, scoop out the flesh into the couscous mixture, mash together with a fork, season and then load back into the aubergine skins.

Return to the oven for a further 5–10 minutes until warmed through, then serve with green salad and scattered with herbs.

SALSA VERDE SWEET POTATOES

Fresh, fragrant and moreish, salsa verde should be your go-to condiment for using up any herbs you have lurking in the refrigerator.

SERVES 4

4 sweet potatoes
2 tablespoons olive oil
salt and pepper
Vegan 'Parmesan' (optional,
   see page 111), to serve

Salsa verde
large handful of soft herb
   leaves, such as basil, mint,
   oregano or parsley, plus
   extra to serve
finely grated zest and juice of
   1 lemon
1 tablespoon capers, drained
2 garlic cloves
2 teaspoons Dijon mustard
2 teaspoons red wine vinegar
50 ml (2 fl oz) olive oil

Preheat the oven to 220°C (425°F), Gas Mark 7.

Hasselback the sweet potatoes by slicing them at 3 mm (⅛ inch) intervals along their length, but not all the way through, so the sweet potato stays connected.

Drizzle with the olive oil, season well and roast for 25 minutes until tender.

Meanwhile, whizz all the ingredients for the salsa verde together in a blender. Season to taste – it should be sharp and lively.

Serve the baked sweet potatoes drizzled with plenty of salsa verde and showered in Vegan 'Parmesan' and herbs, if you like.

SPICED MUSHROOM WRAPS

These spicy mushrooms are completely addictive – this recipe makes more sauce than you need, but you'll want to put it on everything. Alternatively, you could swap it for a shop-bought jerk barbecue sauce to make the whole thing even speedier.

SERVES 4

500 g (1 lb) portobello
    mushrooms, sliced
3 tablespoons olive oil
4 large tortilla wraps

Sauce
½ red onion, roughly
    chopped
2–4 scotch bonnet peppers
    or red chillies
leaves from 5 thyme sprigs
2 tablespoons tomato purée
3 garlic cloves
4 spring onions, roughly
    chopped
4 tablespoons white wine
    vinegar
4 tablespoons soy sauce
10 g (¼ oz) fresh root ginger,
    roughly chopped
2 tablespoons brown sugar
juice of 1 lime
½ teaspoon grated nutmeg
½ teaspoon ground cinnamon
1 tablespoon pepper

Extras (optional)
lettuce
red onion, finely sliced
yellow peppers, sliced
small handful of coriander
    leaves, roughly chopped
mango or pineapple, finely
    chopped

Preheat the oven to 200°C (400°F), Gas Mark 6.

Toss the mushroom slices in the oil on a large baking tray and roast for 20–25 minutes until they have significantly shrunk and browned.

Meanwhile, blitz all the ingredients for the sauce in a blender, starting with the smaller amount of chillies and working your way up.

Toss the cooked mushrooms in the sauce and divide between the wraps with the optional extras of your choice.

WARM KALE & BUTTER BEAN SALAD

This warm salad can take on a multitude of flavours – use the dressing I've given, or invent your own.

SERVES 2

3 tablespoons olive oil

2 shallots, finely sliced

2 garlic cloves, finely grated

400 g (13 oz) can of butter beans, drained and rinsed

200 g (7 oz) cavolo nero, ribs removed, leaves roughly torn

salt and pepper

Zingy shallot dressing

1 shallot, very finely chopped

½ garlic clove, finely grated

2 tablespoons red wine vinegar

1 tablespoon Dijon mustard

2 teaspoons maple syrup or sugar

4 tablespoons olive oil

Heat the oil in a large high-sided frying pan. Add the shallots and cook for 3–5 minutes until softened. Add the garlic and cook until fragrant, around 1 minute. Add the butter beans and cook for 2 minutes until warmed through, followed by the cavolo nero. Cook until wilted – around 3 minutes. Season well.

Mix together all the ingredients for the dressing.

Take off the heat and stir the dressing through the kale and beans. Serve with crusty bread or croutons.

STALK & LENTIL TACOS

Grating broccoli and cauliflower stalks gives an amazing texture to this taco filling. You could use all broccoli, or all cauliflower, or combine them both.

SERVES 6

1 tablespoon olive oil

1 red onion, finely sliced

1 broccoli stalk, grated

1 cauliflower stalk, grated

400g (13 oz) can of green
 lentils in water, drained

2 tablespoons tomato purée

2 teaspoons garlic powder

1 teaspoon smoked paprika

1 teaspoon ground cumin

2 teaspoons vegan bouillon
 powder

200 ml (7 fl oz) water

1 teaspoon hot sauce, or to
 taste

½ teaspoon celery salt, or to
 taste

salt and pepper

Quick red onion pickles

1 red onion, very finely sliced

2 tablespoons white wine
 vinegar or lime juice

pinch of salt

pinch of sugar

Coriander salsa

small bunch of coriander

finely grated zest and juice
 of 1 lime

1 green chilli

1 small garlic clove

To serve

12 small tortillas or hard shell
 tacos

¼ iceberg lettuce, shredded
 (optional)

small handful of coriander
 leaves (optional)

1 lime, cut into wedges

1–2 sliced green chillies
 or pickled jalapeños
 (optional)

For the pickles, in a small bowl, cover the red onion in vinegar or lime juice and add the salt and sugar. Scrunch everything together with your hands – or mix well with a spoon – and set aside for at least 15 minutes. You will see that the onion changes to a pink hue, then they're ready.

Put the oil and red onion in a large frying pan. Add the grated stalks and lentils and cook for 5 minutes until beginning to soften.

Add the tomato purée and seasonings and cook for 1 minute before adding the bouillon powder and measured water. Cook until tender, 5–10 minutes. Season well with hot sauce, celery salt and pepper.

Meanwhile, for the salsa, finely chop the coriander, stalks and all, and mix with the lime zest and juice, chilli and garlic. Loosen with a few tablespoons of water or oil if necessary. Season well and use immediately.

Serve the broccoli lentil mixture on top of tortillas with shredded lettuce, coriander and lime wedges, if using, the onion pickles and coriander salsa.

SWEET POTATO 'CARBONARA' WITH KALE 'BACON'

Try making this creamy pasta with carrots or butternut squash instead of sweet potatoes, and garnishing with crispy sage leaves instead of kale.

SERVES 6

2 sweet potatoes (total weight 350–400 g/ 11½–13 oz)
2 tablespoons olive oil
1 onion, finely chopped
3 garlic cloves, finely grated
1 tablespoon vegan bouillon powder
2 tablespoons nutritional yeast
400 g (13 oz) spaghetti
juice of ½ lemon

Kale 'bacon'
100–150 g (3½–5 oz) kale, ribs removed, leaves roughly torn
1–2 tablespoons olive oil
½ teaspoon granulated or demarara sugar
1 teaspoon smoked paprika
½ teaspoon garlic powder
salt and pepper

Preheat the oven to 220°C (425°F), Gas Mark 7.

Prick the sweet potatoes with a fork all over and microwave on high for 7–8 minutes until tender to the touch.

In the meantime, set a large frying pan over a medium heat, add the oil and onion and cook for 5 minutes until translucent. Add the garlic and cook until fragrant, around 1 minute. Scoop the flesh from the sweet potatoes, mash roughly with a fork and add to the pan. Mix in the bouillon powder and nutritional yeast, then take off the heat.

Meanwhile, boil the pasta for 8–10 minutes until al dente. Reserve 200 ml (7 fl oz) starchy pasta water as it's cooking.

Meanwhile, toss the kale with the oil, sugar and seasonings and roast for 10 minutes until crisp – keep an eye on the leaves, as they can burn easily.

When the pasta is al dente, add the reserved pasta water to the sweet potato pan. Use a stick blender to make the sauce smooth, season with lemon juice, then toss in the spaghetti.

Serve the creamy spaghetti with the crispy kale 'bacon'.

KALE & LENTIL BURGERS

Full of greens and all the good stuff, these burgers make fast food feel like the best food.

SERVES 4

100 g (3½ oz) kale, ribs
    removed, leaves roughly
    torn
15 g (½ oz) chives
50 g (2 oz) gram flour
50 g (2 oz) breadcrumbs
300 g (10 oz) canned green
    lentils or black beans,
    drained and rinsed
100 g (3½ oz) mushrooms
4 tablespoons nutritional
    yeast
1 teaspoon smoked paprika
2 tablespoons olive oil
salt and pepper

To serve
burger buns
lettuce
tomatoes
vegan mayo (for homemade
    see page 15, optional)
mustard (optional)

Put all the ingredients for the patties except the olive oil in a blender and blitz together. Season well.

Form the mixture into 4 patties.

Heat the oil in a large frying pan and fry the burgers for 3 minutes on each side until golden and crisp.

Serve with the burger buns and the toppings of your choice.

SWEET POTATO BURGERS

I love to make these burgers with leftover rice, but if you don't have any then a microwaveable packet of rice can really speed things up. Feel free to pimp your burgers with whatever toppings you like – pickles, hot sauce, sliced red onion – whatever you fancy. You can also mix vegan mayo with some sriracha sauce for a quick burger sauce.

MAKES 4-6

400 g (13 oz) sweet potato
100 g (3½ oz) black beans
   (drained weight), drained
   and rinse
150 g (5 oz) cooked rice
2 spring onions, finely sliced
1 teaspoon ground cumin
½ teaspoon smoked paprika
2 tablespoons flavourless oil
salt and pepper

To serve
4-6 burger buns
1 large tomato, sliced
4-6 lettuce leaves
½ red onion, sliced (optional)

Prick the sweet potato all over and microwave on high for 7–8 minutes until tender.

In the meantime, put the black beans in a large bowl. Mash them roughly with a fork. Add the rice, spring onions and seasonings and mix well.

Scoop the flesh from the sweet potatoes and add to the bowl, mash with the back of a fork and stir well to combine.

Form the mixture into 4–6 patties, depending on the size of your burger buns.

Heat the oil in a large frying pan and fry the burger patties for 2–3 minutes on each side until golden and crisp.

Serve in burger buns with tomato, lettuce and any other toppings of your choice.

BLACK BEAN MEATBALLS

SERVES 4–6

2 x 400 g (13 oz) cans of
black beans, drained and
rinsed

1 red onion, roughly chopped

1 teaspoon garlic powder

½ teaspoon chilli flakes

1 teaspoon dried oregano

2 tablespoons nutritional
yeast

8 tablespoons breadcrumbs

2 tablespoons flavourless oil

Tomato sauce

3 tablespoons olive oil

3 garlic cloves, finely sliced

500 ml (17 fl oz) tomato
passata

1 teaspoon Marmite or other
yeast extract

½ teaspoon sugar (optional)

salt and pepper

These soft meatballs are so easy to whip up – they're not that delicate when frying, but when simmering them in the sauce, be careful not to agitate the pan too much because you don't want them to fall apart. The Marmite in the tomato sauce gives it that slow-cooked savoury meatiness that all meatballs deserve. You can swap the black beans for kidney beans or chickpeas, if you prefer. Serve with spaghetti and lots of basil.

Blitz the black beans, red onion, seasonings and breadcrumbs in a food processor until you have a rough paste. Shape the burgers into golf-sized balls and set aside on a tray.

For the sauce, heat the olive oil in a high-sided frying pan and add the garlic. Cook for 1–2 minutes until fragrant and just about to be golden. Add the passata, Marmite and sugar, if using, season, and simmer for 15 minutes until reduced.

In a separate frying pan, heat the flavourless oil over a medium heat. Fry the meatballs in batches, taking care not to overcrowd the pan, until golden and crisp all over.

Carefully transfer the meatballs to the sauce, cover and simmer for 5 minutes, then serve.

BLACK BEAN MEATBALL SUB

MAKES 4

4 soft rolls or hot dog buns

½ quantity Black Bean
Meatballs (above)

4 tablespoons crispy onions

large handful of basil leaves

Vegan 'Parmesan' (optional)

70 g (2¾ oz) cashews,
peanuts or flaked almonds

3 tablespoons nutritional
yeast

½ teaspoon salt

I think it's completely justifiable to make a batch of these meatballs purely so you can enjoy this indulgent treat.

Preheat the grill to high.

Whizz everything for the Vegan 'Parmesan', if making, together in a blender until it resembles sand or breadcrumbs. Set aside.

Split open the rolls or buns and add a single layer of meatballs in sauce to each.

Place under the grill for 5 minutes until the filling is bubbling and the sides of the bread are toasted. Sprinkle with the crispy onions, basil leaves and Vegan 'Parmesan', if using, then serve.

SMOKY MUSHROOM BOWLS

This works with any kind of mushroom, but if you can find them at your local greengrocer then I think oyster mushrooms have the best texture. Add any toppings and sides you have hanging around – these bowls are great with pitta breads or wraps, chilli sauce, olives, pickles or an extra drizzle of tahini.

SERVES 4–6

Mushrooms
1 kg (2 lb) oyster mushrooms, roughly sliced
½ teaspoon ground turmeric
1 teaspoon smoked paprika
1 teaspoon ground cumin
½ teaspoon ground cinnamon
3 tablespoons olive oil
2 tablespoons soy sauce
1 tablespoon maple syrup

Bowls
1 cucumber, chopped
200 g (7 oz) cherry tomatoes, halved
1 red onion, finely sliced
finely grated zest and juice of 1 lemon
200 g (7 oz) hummus
1 Romaine heart or ½ iceberg lettuce, shredded
small handful of parsley and mint leaves
salt and pepper

Toss the mushrooms with the spices. Preheat a large frying pan and add the oil and mushrooms. Fry for 10–15 minutes until soft and brown. Splash in the soy sauce and maple syrup.

While the mushrooms are cooking, mix together the cucumber, tomatoes, red onion and lemon zest and juice. Season well.

Divide the hummus between 4–6 bowls and top with the mushrooms. Serve with the shredded lettuce and chopped cucumber and tomato, sprinkled with fresh herbs.

BALSAMIC MUSHROOMS WITH SPINACH

This is a lovely treat, or for a bit of extra indulgence, try serving it with rice, stirring a generous amount of tahini through the rice first until its creamy and gooey.

SERVES 2-4

2 tablespoons vegan butter
1 red onion, finely sliced
5 garlic cloves, finely sliced
2 tablespoons balsamic
    vinegar
1 tablespoon brown sugar
100 g (3½ oz) sun-dried
    tomatoes
400 g (13 oz) chestnut
    button mushrooms, halved
200 g (7 oz) spinach
salt and pepper
1 tablespoon finely chopped
    chives, to serve

Melt the vegan butter in a large frying pan. Add the onion and cook for 5 minutes until translucent. Add the garlic and cook for another minute until fragrant. Add the balsamic vinegar and sugar, reduce the heat to its lowest, and leave to caramelize – 8–10 minutes.

Add the sun-dried tomatoes and mushrooms and cook for 10–15 minutes until the mushrooms have released all their moisture. Add the spinach, allow to wilt, then season to taste. Serve sprinkled with chives.

SLOPPY SWEET POTATO CHILLI

Both the mushrooms and dried mushrooms here give a delectable depth to this chilli. It freezes nicely, so either make it for a crowd or stash your leftovers for a lazy evening. This chilli uses celery salt to add another layer to the seasoning.

SERVES 6

2 x 400 g (13 oz) cans of
   black beans, drained and
   rinsed
200 g (7 oz) can of
   sweetcorn, drained
200 g (7 oz) mushrooms
15 g (½ oz) dried mushrooms
   (optional)
2 tablespoons olive oil
1 red onion, finely chopped
3 garlic cloves, finely grated
1 tablespoon chipotle paste
1 teaspoon smoked paprika
1 teaspoon celery salt
1 tablespoon Marmite or
   other yeast extract
2–3 sweet potatoes (total
   weight about 500 g/1 lb),
   peeled and chopped into
   small cubes
2 x 400 g (13 oz) cans of
   chopped tomatoes
250 ml (8 fl oz) vegetable
   stock
salt and pepper

In a food processor, blitz together half the black beans, the sweetcorn, mushrooms and dried mushrooms, if using, until you have a rough paste. Set aside.

Put the olive oil in a large heavy-based saucepan and add the onion and garlic. Cook for 5 minutes until soft, then add the bean and mushroom paste along with the seasonings, sweet potatoes and remaining black beans. Cook for 2 minutes, then add the canned tomatoes and stock. Simmer for 20–25 minutes until the sauce has thickened and the sweet potato is tender.

Season to taste.

SLOPPY JOES

SERVES 4

1 green pepper, finely
    chopped
1 tablespoon olive oil
½ quantity Sloppy Sweet
    Potato Chilli (see page 115)
2 teaspoons American
    mustard
2 teaspoons tomato ketchup

To serve
¼ white cabbage, grated
¼ red cabbage, grated
1 carrot, grated
finely grated zest and juice
    of 1 lime
4 burger buns
large handful of pickled
    jalapeños
salt and pepper

Yes, adding ketchup and mustard seems like a strange thing to do, but no, you won't regret it.

Put the green pepper and oil into a frying pan and sauté for 5 minutes until softened. Add the Chilli and bring to the boil, adding a splash of water to loosen if needed. Add the mustard and ketchup and cook for 5 minutes further.

Toss the grated cabbage and carrot with the lime zest and juice in a large bowl. Season well.

Assemble the sloppy joes by loading the Chilli on to the burger buns and topping with slaw and pickled jalapeños.

LOADED SLOPPY FRIES

SERVES 2–4

250 g (8 oz) oven chips
½ quantity Sloppy Sweet
    Potato Chilli (see page 115)
1 avocado, chopped
½ red onion, very finely
    chopped
large handful of coriander
    leaves
25 g (1 oz) crispy onions
salt and pepper

A perfect way to use up any leftover chilli, these do live up to their name in the mess department.

Preheat the oven to 220°C (425°F), Gas Mark 7 and cook the oven chips according to the packet instructions – typically 20 minutes.

Warm the Chilli in a saucepan over a low heat until piping hot throughout. When the chips are cooked, transfer them to a serving platter, spoon the Chilli over and load up with avocado, red onion, coriander and crispy onions. Season and serve.

ROASTED SWEETHEART CABBAGE ON QUICK POLENTA

Quick-cook polenta is a godsend. It take a fraction of the time of authentic polenta to cook – which means less stirring, and more enjoying. I love to add a good drizzle of olive oil on top to finish it off. The cabbage here has so much flavour itself, that, when roasted, it really needs nothing more than oil, salt and pepper to taste smoky, sweet and savoury.

SERVES 4

1 sweetheart cabbage,
   quartered or cut into 8,
   depending on size
2 tablespoons olive oil
salt and pepper

Polenta
800 ml (1 pint 3½ fl oz)
   vegetable stock
200 g (7 oz) quick-cook
   polenta
2 tablespoons nutritional
   yeast
4 tablespoons vegan butter

To serve (optional)
1 teaspoon chilli flakes
2 tablespoons flaked almonds
A small handful of parsley,
   leaves only
1 lemon, cut into wedges

Preheat the oven to 200°C (400°F), Gas Mark 6.

Toss the cabbage with the oil and season well, then lay it on a baking tray and roast for 20–25 minutes until charred and blistered.

Meanwhile, pour the stock into a saucepan and bring to the boil. Pour in the polenta in a steady stream, whisking constantly. Keep whisking until the mixture comes back to the boil, then reduce the heat to as low as it will go and simmer, stirring regularly, for 5 minutes.

Stir through the nutritional yeast and vegan butter and season well.

Serve the polenta immediately, topped with the roasted cabbage, chilli flakes, almonds and parsley scattered over, if using, and with the lemon wedges on the side.

BANG BANG BROCCOLI

'Bang bang' was originally named because of the bashing needed to tenderize the meat the original recipe contained, but it seems just as apt for the slap-in-the-face bangin' spice that this sauce brings to things. Swap the broccoli for cauliflower, or even asparagus if you have some.

SERVES 2 OR 4 AS A SIDE

1 head of broccoli, broken into florets
4 tablespoons cornflour
2 teaspoons garlic powder
1 teaspoon chilli powder
4 tablespoons dairy-free milk
100 g (3½ oz) breadcrumbs
4 tablespoons flavourless oil
salt and pepper
1 tablespoon sesame seeds, to serve

Bang bang sauce
3 tablespoons vegan mayo (for homemade see page 15)
2 tablespoons sriracha or chilli sauce
1 tablespoon maple syrup or sugar

Preheat the oven to 220°C (425°F), Gas Mark 7.

Put the broccoli on a large baking tray. Sprinkle with the cornflour and spices and toss to coat. Pour over the dairy-free milk and toss to coat again, followed by the breadcrumbs, tossing once more. Season well.

Drizzle the oil over the florets and bake for 15–20 minutes until the breadcrumbs are deeply golden.

While the broccoli is cooking, mix together the vegan mayo, sriracha and syrup to make the bang bang sauce.

To serve, cover the broccoli in the bang bang sauce and sprinkle with sesame seeds.

SPEEDY SWEETS

BAKED TAHINI BANANAS

This lovely recipe works really well with peanut butter instead of tahini,
and even better served with a big scoop of vegan ice cream.

SERVES 2

2 unpeeled bananas
handful of mixed nuts (try
    walnuts and hazelnuts),
    roughly chopped
4 squares of dark chocolate
1 tablespoon tahini
1 tablespoon pomegranate
    seeds (optional), to serve

Preheat the oven to 160°C (325°F), Gas Mark 3.

Bake the bananas in their skins on a baking tray for
15 minutes.

Once the skins are black, use a knife to slice down the
middle of the bananas.

Stuff the nuts and chocolate inside and bake for
10 minutes more until the chocolate is melted and gooey.

Drizzle with tahini, scatter with pomegranate seeds,
if using, and serve.

RASPBERRY & CHOCOLATE MICROWAVE COOKIE

Once you discover the joy of a microwave cookie, you'll never go back.
Be warned, when it's just cooked, it will be squishy and volcanically hot,
so it's best to wait a few minutes after cooking, until the edges get crispy
and the middle sets, before diving in.

MAKES 1

2 tablespoons vegan butter

2½ tablespoons light brown
  sugar

5 tablespoons plain flour

pinch of salt

2–3 raspberries, quartered or
  halved

6–10 vegan chocolate
  chips or 2 squares of
  dark chocolate, roughly
  chopped

Put the butter in a small microwave-safe bowl and microwave for 1 minute on high until melted.

Stir in the sugar, flour and salt until a thick dough forms. Fold in half the raspberries and chocolate chips.

Scrape the mixture on to a microwave-safe plate and form it into a round thick cookie 'puck' shape with your hands. Arrange the remaining raspberries and chocolate on top (this is purely visual, so don't worry if you can't squeeze them on).

Microwave for 1 minute 30 seconds on high until the cookie has spread and cracked slightly, looks like it is beginning to firm up on top and you can see that the chocolate is melty.

Allow to cool and set up for 5 minutes before eating.

PORRIDGE OAT BARS

These cake-like oat bars are best baked in the oven, but can also be ready in 3–5 minutes on high in the microwave – they'll just have a slightly denser texture. Make them with any lurking berries in the refrigerator, or grated apple also works a treat. They're infinitely customizable.

MAKES 4

75 g (3 oz) oats
150 ml (¼ pint) dairy-free milk
1 banana
1 tablespoon sweetener of your choice, such as brown sugar, maple syrup or golden syrup
1 teaspoon baking powder

Preheat the oven to 180°C (350°F), Gas Mark 4.

Blitz all the ingredients together in a blender until smooth.

Pour the batter into a small ovenproof dish (about 16 x 12 cm/6½ x 5 inches), or smaller individual ramekins, and bake for 15–20 minutes until risen, golden and firm.

BERRY BLACK FOREST

1 quantity Porridge Oat
Bars batter, uncooked
(see page 126)
4 squares of dark chocolate
small handful of berries (try
cherries, blackberries or
raspberries)

Frozen berries would work great here as well and are much cheaper than fresh.

After pouring the batter into the dish, nestle the chocolate and berries on top and bake as directed in the main recipe.

CARROT CAKE

1 quantity Porridge Oat Bars
batter, uncooked
(see page 126)
½ carrot, finely grated
½ teaspoon ground cinnamon
½ teaspoon mixed spice

This brings some warming spice into the mix, very comforting and incredibly tasty.

After blitzing together the base recipe, stir through the grated carrot and spices. Bake as directed in the main recipe.

PEANUT BUTTER & JELLY

1 quantity Porridge Oat Bars
batter, uncooked
(see page 126)
1 tablespoon peanut butter
1 tablespoon raspberry (or
any flavour) jam
2 tablespoons raw peanuts,
roughly chopped

You can't beat this classic combination; feel free to use any kind of jam here.

After pouring the batter into the dish, drizzle the peanut butter and jam over the surface and use the back of a spoon to marble them together. Sprinkle with peanuts and bake as directed in the main recipe.

APPLE FRITTERS

These are based on a drop doughnut-style recipe. They are also really nice tossed in cinnamon sugar and served with dark chocolate sauce, as if they were churros. If you don't have an apple corer, use a small sharp knife to bore into the fruit and remove the cores in a single piece.

SERVES 4–6

3 apples, peeled and cored
200 g (7 oz) plain flour
1 teaspoon baking powder
1½ tablespoons caster sugar
1 teaspoon vanilla extract
   (optional)
200 ml (7 fl oz) dairy-free
   milk
flavourless oil, to deep-fry
2 tablespoons icing sugar

Slice the apples 1 cm (½ inch) thick and set aside.

Use a whisk to combine the plain flour, baking powder and caster sugar in a bowl. Slowly add the vanilla, if using, and dairy-free milk and whisk until you have a smooth batter.

Bring the oil to 170°C (340°F) in a deep saucepan or wok. If you don't have a thermometer, throw in a drop of batter: it should sizzle, but not turn golden immediately. Dip the apple slices into the batter, coating well, then lower straight into the oil (taking care to not burn yourself – use a fork) and cook for 2–3 minutes until golden and puffy. You will need to cook them in smallish batches of 3–4 at a time, to avoid overcrowding the pan.

Remove with a slotted spoon and drain on a piece of kitchen paper. Sift the icing sugar over the top and serve immediately.

MILK & COOKIE BROWNIES

This is a pretty easy formula to remember for the easiest and fudgiest brownies – equal weights of pretty much any cookies and milk with a dash of baking powder. Add a twist with a few chocolate chunks or nuts, or marble the surface with vegan white chocolate or peanut butter. Wonderful with fresh fruit or ice cream.

MAKES 8 BROWNIES

300 g (10 oz) chocolate
    sandwich cookies, such as
    Oreos, plus 5 extra, roughly
    chopped (optional)
300 ml (½ pint) dairy-free
    milk
1½ teaspoons baking powder

Preheat the oven to 180°C (350°F), Gas Mark 4. Line the base of a 22 x 18 cm (8½ x 7 inch) cake tin with baking paper.

Blitz the cookies in a food processor to a fine crumb, then add the milk and baking powder and blitz until smooth.

Pour the batter into the prepared tin and top with the extra chopped cookies, if using. Bake for 15 minutes, or until a skewer inserted in the centre comes out clean. Allow to cool before slicing into 8.

CARAMEL CITRUS SALAD

This is an incredibly easy dinner-party dessert – just the tangy, tart sort of thing people fancy after a big meal. Make it ahead and let it sit and get lovely and crunchy. You want to get the colour of the caramel quite dark here as the deep, almost bitter caramel flavour really complements the sharp oranges. To wash up the pan, bring some water to the boil in it, to dissolve any set caramel.

SERVES 4–6

6 assorted oranges (such as
    clementines, oranges or
    blood oranges)
1 grapefruit
150 g (5 oz) caster sugar
a few mint leaves, to serve

Use a serrated knife to peel the oranges and grapefruit, cutting away all the white pith and membrane. Slice into rounds and arrange on a platter.

Heat a wide heavy-based pan over a medium heat for 2 minutes. Add the sugar and 3 tablespoons of water.

Allow the sugar to dissolve in the water, then let the mixture gently come up to a boil; don't stir it. Cook for 6–8 minutes until the caramel is a deep shade of amber. Pour the caramel over the citrus straight away and allow to set (around 10 minutes).

Just before serving, sprinkle with mint leaves.

BROKE 'CHURROS'

It helps here if your bread is stale, because it turns crispy more quickly, but of course just use whatever you have. Don't forget: cheap, white sliced bread is key here, because it's so cakey anyway.

SERVES 4

1 teaspoon ground cinnamon
100 g (3½ oz) granulated
   sugar
100 g (3½ oz) dark chocolate,
   broken into squares
4 slices of stale white
   sliced bread
4 tablespoons vegan butter

In a shallow bowl, mix together the cinnamon and sugar. Set aside.

Melt the chocolate in 30-second increments in the microwave on high until smooth. Set aside.

Slice the bread into thick strips.

Heat 2 tablespoons of the vegan butter in a large frying pan and cook half the bread strips for 1–2 minutes on each side until toasty and golden. Remove from the pan, add straight to the cinnamon sugar bowl and toss to coat.

Repeat with the remaining vegan butter and bread strips. Serve dunked in the melted chocolate.

CORNFLAKE NUTTY FINGERS

These are like a grown-up cereal treat bar. The bars are deliberately spread quite thin, so they only need a little while to set in the freezer to make sure the chocolate hardens.

SERVES 4

4 squares of dark chocolate
30 g (1 oz) cornflakes
100 g (3½ oz) peanut butter
1 tablespoon sweetener of your choice (such as maple syrup, golden syrup or brown sugar)

Melt the chocolate in 30-second increments in the microwave on high until smooth. Set aside.

Put the cornflakes in a resealable food bag and bash a few times with a rolling pin until you have some fine crumbs and some larger pieces. Pour into a bowl and mix with the peanut butter and sweetener.

Spread the mixture out in between 2 pieces of nonstick baking parchment, until 1–2cm (½–¾ inch) thick. Peel back the top layer of paper and drizzle the melted chocolate on top and freeze for 10–15 minutes.

Slice into bars and serve. You can store these in the refrigerator or freezer – up to you.

CHOCOLATE CRACKLE SHELL

This is the quickest-to-make chocolate sauce I know to pour over ice cream. Leave it for a few minutes and it'll make a hard shell that you can crack through for all the crunchy satisfaction.

SERVES 4–6

2 tablespoons coconut oil
1 tablespoon cocoa powder
1 teaspoon golden syrup

Melt the coconut oil in a microwave on high, or in a saucepan, then whisk in the cocoa powder and golden syrup.

Serve on top of ice cream, a smoothie bowl or indeed anything chilled.

STEAMED PUDDINGS

GOLDEN SYRUP

SERVES 4

vegan margarine, for the
    mould(s)
6 tablespoons golden syrup
75 g (3 oz) caster sugar
75 g (3 oz) vegetable oil
150 g (5 oz) self-raising flour
125 ml (4 fl oz) dairy-free
    milk
½ tablespoon apple cider
    vinegar or white wine
    vinegar
1 teaspoon baking powder
pinch of salt

*Steamed sponges taste incredibly nostalgic to me, and
I couldn't believe it when I found they could be made in
a microwave. Game. Changer. These are really lovely as
individual puddings, so it's worth buying some cheap plastic
moulds, but if you only have one large microwave-safe bowl,
make a large pudding and add change the cooking time to
5–6 minutes.*

Grease 4 microwave-safe individual pudding moulds
(approximately 150 ml/¼ pint in size) well with margarine.
Divide the golden syrup between the moulds and set aside.

In a separate bowl, mix together all the remaining ingredients,
then divide between the prepared moulds.

Cover the pudding moulds with clingfilm and microwave one
at a time on high for 1 minute 30 seconds. Leave to stand for
5 minutes before turning out on a plate – it can help to loosen
the edges with a knife.

MARMALADE

SERVES 4

vegan margarine, for the
    mould(s)
4 tablespoons marmalade
75 g (3 oz) caster sugar
75 g (3 oz) vegetable oil
150 g (5 oz) self-raising flour
125 ml (4 fl oz) dairy-free
    milk
finely grated zest of 1 orange
1 tablespoon orange juice
1 teaspoon baking powder
pinch of salt

*The tanginess of the marmalade sets off the sweetness of the
pudding beautifully here.*

Follow the directions in the main recipe (above), but instead
of golden syrup, divide the marmalade between the moulds
before filling. Add the orange zest to the batter.

Bake as directed.

BERRY

SERVES 4

This fruity variation adds a welcome sharpness from the jam as well as a hint of citrus from the lemon zest.

---

vegan margarine, for the
    mould(s)
4 tablespoons raspberry or
    strawberry jam
75 g (3 oz) caster sugar
75 g (3 oz) vegetable oil
150 g (5 oz) self-raising flour
125 ml (4 fl oz) dairy-free
    milk
finely grated zest of 1 lemon
1 tablespoon lemon juice
1 teaspoon baking powder
pinch of salt

Follow the directions in the main recipe (see page 136), but instead of golden syrup, divide the jam between the moulds before filling. Add the lemon zest to the batter.

Bake as directed.

QUICK COFFEE CUPCAKES

The absolute perfect bite of cake with your coffee. This is a chuck-it-all-in-one-bowl type of baking. The icing is optional, not only because these are delicious on their own, but because in order to ice the cupcakes I do recommend that you wait until they are cool – which, depending on how cool your kitchen is, might take a little longer.

MAKES 12

160 g (5½ oz) plain flour

150 g (5 oz) light brown sugar

1 teaspoon bicarbonate of soda

½ teaspoon ground cinnamon

pinch of salt

2 tablespoons instant coffee powder

150 ml (¼ pint) dairy-free milk

100 ml (3½ fl oz) flavourless oil

1 tablespoon apple cider vinegar

Icing (optional)
150 g (5 oz) icing sugar
60 g (2¼ oz) vegan butter
½ tablespoon instant coffee powder
1 teaspoon vanilla extract (optional)
handful of walnuts (optional)

Preheat the oven to 180°C (350°F), Gas Mark 4. Line a muffin or cupcake tray with 12 cupcake cases.

Put the flour, sugar, bicarbonate of soda, cinnamon, salt and coffee powder in a bowl and whisk to combine.

Add the milk, oil and vinegar and whisk thoroughly to combine until it is a smooth batter. Fill the cupcake cases two-thirds of the way and bake for 12–15 minutes until golden and risen.

Remove from the tray and allow to cool on a wire rack (ideally outside or somewhere cold) for 10 minutes.

Meanwhile, if icing, cream the icing sugar, butter and coffee powder together until smooth and creamy, adding the vanilla, if you want. Add a little dollop to each cupcake, top with a walnut, if you like, and enjoy.

SPEEDY CINNAMON ROLLS

*These feel equally appropriate at breakfast time as for a sweet treat –
and they're so quick to make that there's really no reason not to try 'em.*

MAKES 2

1 banana

12 tablespoons plain flour,
    plus extra for dusting

2 teaspoons baking powder

1–4 tablespoons dairy-free
    milk

2 tablespoons granulated
    sugar

1 teaspoon ground cinnamon

1 tablespoon vegan butter,
    melted

Glaze

100 g (3½ oz) icing sugar

1–2 tablespoons dairy-free
    milk

In a large bowl, mash the banana with a fork, then add
the flour, baking powder and milk and bring together into
a thick, slightly tacky dough.

Lightly flour a work surface and push the dough out
with your hands until you have a thick rectangle about
20 x 30 cm (8 x 12 inches) large.

Combine the granulated sugar and cinnamon, then
brush the dough with the melted butter and sprinkle the
cinnamon sugar on top. Roll up tightly from the long edge
to make a spiralled log.

Slice the dough log into 5–6 and nestle the rolls into
2 mugs or a small microwave-safe dish. Microwave on high
for 2–3 minutes if in a single dish, or 1 minute 30 seconds
for each mug, until puffy and golden.

While the cinnamon rolls are cooking, mix together the
icing sugar and dairy-free milk until you have a smooth
dropping consistency. Pour over the cinnamon rolls
and enjoy.

FLOURLESS CHOCOLATE & BANANA BAKE

Some sort of sorcery happens in the oven here to create the fudgiest, squidgiest, most indulgent dessert you've ever tried. Somewhere between a brownie, a lava cake and a fondant, this is a new category of its own. Serve with a big scoop of vegan ice cream.

SERVES 4–6

5–6 ripe bananas, depending on size

200 g (7 oz) peanut butter

50 g (2 oz) cocoa powder

½ tablespoon bicarbonate of soda

70 ml (2¾ fl oz) golden syrup or maple syrup

100 g (3½ oz) chocolate chunks or dark chocolate, roughly chopped (optional)

Preheat the oven to 180°C (350°F), Gas Mark 4. Line the base of a 22 x 18 cm (8½ x 7 inch) cake tin with baking paper.

In a large bowl, mash the bananas thoroughly. Mix in the peanut butter, cocoa powder, bicarbonate of soda and syrup. Fold through the chocolate chunks, if using.

Bake for 15–20 minutes until firm to the touch on top.

Scoop out portions and serve with ice cream.

INDEX

UK/US GLOSSARY

UK	US
Aubergine	Eggplant
Baking paper	Parchment paper
Beetroot	Beet
Bicarbonate of soda	Baking soda
Blitz/Whizz	To process in a food processor or blender
Borlotti beans	Cranberry beans
Bouillon cube/powder	Stock cube/powder
Butter beans	Lima beans
Caster sugar	Superfine sugar
Cavolo nero	Tuscan kale (black kale)
Chestnut mushroom	Cremini mushroom
Chips	Fries
Clingfilm	Plastic wrap
Coriander	Cilantro (but coriander if the seed, whole or ground)
Cornflour	Cornstarch
Courgette	Zucchini
Dark chocolate	Semisweet chocolate
Double cream	Heavy cream
Flaked almonds	Slivered or sliced almonds
Golden syrup	Light corn syrup
Gram flour	Chickpea (besan) flour
High-sided frying pan	Deep skillet
Icing sugar	Confectioners' sugar
Jacket potato	Baked potato
Kitchen paper	Paper towels
Pak choi	Bok choy

UK	US
Plain flour	All-purpose flour
Pulses	Legumes (beans, chickpeas, and lentils)
Self-raising flour	Use all-purpose flour plus 2 teaspoons baking per 125 g/1 cup of flour (note that UK self-raising flour is not the same as the US self-rising flour)
Sieve	Strainer
Soda water	Club soda
Spring onion	Scallion
Starter	Appetizer
Stick blender	Immersion blender
Storecupboard	Pantry
Sultanas	Golden raisins
Sweetcorn, canned	Corn kernels
Tea towel	Dish towel
Tenderstem broccoli	Broccolini (baby broccoli)
Tomato passata	Tomato puree/tomato sauce
Tomato purée	Tomato paste
White cabbage	Green cabbage

Note: UK imperial fluid ounces and US fluid ounces are not the same: 1 ml = US 0.0338 fl oz or UK 0.035 fl oz. For smaller measures, the differences are negligible, but for larger quantities, convert from metric, multiplying them by 0.0338, for a more accurate measurement. In addition, a UK pint = 20 UK fl oz, more than the standard US 16 fl oz (2 cups).